ECSTATIC
CHRISTIANITY

ECSTATIC CHRISTIANITY

MUNDAY MARTIN

FOREWORD BY JAMES W. GOLL

TALL PINE

"Munday Martin is a genuine New Testament evangelist who will boldly go where few would dare go. With courage and compassion, he goes to the streets and schools, parks, and grocery stores, going to any place where he can share the good news of Jesus Christ. The Great Commission is his mandate, and he takes it seriously. Ecstatic Christianity will motivate you and educate you in the ways of evangelism, and written by a true evangelist who is changing the world."

—JEFF JANSEN
Founder of *Global Fire Publishing*
Author of *Trump, The Destiny of God's America* and *Glory Rising*

"One of the greatest lessons that you can learn in this life is to let go and let God. I believe that if you are a follower of Jesus Christ, you are called to walk in supernatural surrender and significance. In this book, Munday Martin challenges the status quo of comfortable Christianity as he invites you to dream with God and believe for the impossible. *Ecstatic Christianity* imparts contagious faith through each chapter. You'll encounter biblical truth along with testimonies of miracles that illustrate a Spirit-filled lifestyle. If you want to see transformation come to your city, join this passionate pursuit of the Great Commission in which all Christians are meant to participate. You'll be encouraged to dive headlong into the river of God and embrace the joy of your new life found in Christ!"

—CHÉ AHN
Founder and President, *Harvest International Ministry*
Founding and Senior Pastor, *Harvest Rock Church* Pasadena, CA

"I want to thank my dear friend, Munday Martin, for allowing me the privilege of writing this endorsement of *Ecstatic Christianity*.

As an evangelist who's been in the ministry for over 16 years and having won 7.25 million people to Christ, I say that this book imparts faith. As Evangelist's our primary call is to impart faith, for we are saved by grace through faith, and this book imparts faith to the readers and inspires them to win the lost and impart faith to them. This book is a fire starter, and it resonates with me and the message I preach.

Specifically, these titles, "Lose My Unbelief," "Find Greater Faith," and "Soul Winner" are some of the key features, in my humble opinion, that tailor-make a great preacher! This book is such a great read! I highly recommend it. I'm so proud of you, my friend! Keep doing the greater things!"

—ANKIT RAMBABU
www.ankitrambabu.org

"My friend, Munday Martin, has written a must-read for anyone passionate about living a radical sold-out life for Jesus. I have personally known Munday for twenty years and can tell you that he lives and breathes what has been written within the pages of this book. Engage this book and expect God to bring you into new dimensions of grace and glory."

—PROPHET CHARLIE SHAMP
Co-Founder of *Destiny Encounters International*

"Jesus told his disciples that they would receive power from on high, and they would be His witnesses to the remotest parts of the earth" (Acts 1:8, NASB).

Ecstatic Christianity shows the purpose of a life filled with power from on high is to experience personal transformation and prophetic power, just like Acts 2, so you can be a passionate witness for Christ. Many people do not see biblical results (healing, miracles, signs, and wonders) because they are not filled with the Holy Spirit. I highly encourage you to read this book and be inspired to receive power from on high. Then you, too, will see many people won to the saving power of Christ."

—STACEY CAMPBELL
Author of *Ecstatic Prophecy* and *Praying the Bible Series*
shilohcompany.org
wesleystaceycampbell.com

"*Ecstatic Christianity* will break any complacency or fear off of you. The Gospel and hope of Jesus are meant to be shared! Munday's faith and raw vulnerability are contagious, and no doubt it's the reason he's making such an impact for the Kingdom of God."

—ANA WERNER
Founder of *Ana Werner Ministries*
President, *Eagles Network*
Author, *The Seer's Path, Seeing Behind the Veil, The Warrior's Dance*,
co-author of *Accessing the Greater Glory*
www.anawerner.org

"I am amazed at the insight Munday Martin has in winning souls. In *Ecstatic Christianity,* he walks you through this process and shows you how to get on fire for God and learn to help others. He takes you from emptiness to losing yourself in Jesus, and to be a Soul Winner! My favorite part is chapter eleven, Juicy Fruit, where Munday shows you how to unlock the Miracle Ministry inside you! Once you start reading this book, you might not be able to put it down. There is so much in here that we, as the body of Christ, need today. After you finish reading this book, you will want to get more copies to share with others."

—IVAN TUTTLE
ivantuttleministries.com

To my Lord and Savior Jesus the Messiah who rescued me when I was going down for the last count. I'm forever indebted to love you and the body of Christ.

To my wife, Jennifer, who is the personification of true loyalty and friendship. You daily help me reach for the stars. That's right!

And to my children, Samuel, who reminds me to laugh, stay childlike, and fear God. and to JennaBeth who teaches me what a pure heart looks like that will see God.

I pray to leave behind a Legacy for all of you that will cause you and all of your families to run after Jesus with all your heart.

"To the Jewish people and the nation of Israel where we spent almost a year of our life doing evangelism. May you come to know Jesus (Yeshua) as the Messiah of Israel and the Gentiles. I am forever indebted to love you!" (Romans 9,10, and 11)

CONTENTS

FOREWORD

I asked myself what three words I would use to describe Munday Martin. I pondered for a moment, not long at all actually, and three words popped right into my mind: Contagious, Adventurous, and Authentic. I invite you to go on a short journey with me as I unpack these three words.

I remember years ago when I was having a meeting with Munday in my home, and we were talking about who he was and what he did and what he wanted to do. I asked him the current name of their ministry, and he told me the name. I thought it sounds interesting, but it just doesn't quite fit. I asked the Holy Spirit, "Who is this guy? What do you think of Him?" Immediately, the Holy Spirit spoke to me, "Oh, Munday is Contagious..." I thought, "Wow, is that ever accurate." The Holy Spirit added, "Munday and Jennifer are all about spreading my love around the world to every person they meet."

I will never forget the day when I looked at Munday in my upper room and said, "Why you are Contagious! Then I spoke.

"The Lord says you are 'Contagious Love International.'" From that moment on, they shifted the name of their ministry to Contagious Love International.

ADVENTUROUS!

I met Munday when he was only 17 years old. He and his prophetic buddy, Charlie Shamp, came to one of our prophetic conferences that Michal Ann and I were hosting in partnership with Mickey and Barbara Robinson. These guys showed up and were hungry for God like crazy. I remember knowing something special about these crazy guys. They were ready for an adventure, and they both are still to this day.

Recently, I did my weekly God Encounters Today Podcast interview with Munday. He was telling me these outrageous stories about preaching the gospel of Jesus over the loudspeaker at a well-known retail outlet. "Anyone need prayer? Come right up here, and I will pray for you. Jesus saved me, and Jesus wants to save you too!" Yes, Munday is contagious, and amazing Munday is also full of new adventures in Christ Jesus!

AUTHENTIC!

There was not one ounce of fake in this guy and he was without pretense or fraud! He loves God. He has had a great relationship with his parents. He is crae crae about his wife Jennifer and when she gets him talking about his two kids, he is a puddle on the floor. When you get him to talk about the lost, you realize he is a weeping intercessor! Munday is the real deal. He is multitalented, and fun. He is full of life and does not have a religious bone in his body. Munday is authentic.

So, you say, what an unusual foreword for a book called *Ecstatic Christianity*. Oh no! This book, which you are holding in your hand, is full of testimonies of God's contagious love. The pages are full invitations to go on adventures into a realm of faith that is absolutely ecstatic! The content you are about to devour is genuine. It comes from someone who lives what he preaches and is an incarnation of authentic Christianity.

It is an honor to love, cheer for, and commend to you the life and ministry and now the writings of my friend and son-in-the faith, Munday Martin. I want to be like him when I grow up. Gospel Truth!

—JAMES W. GOLL
Founder of *God Encounters Ministries*
GOLL Ideation LLC

INTRODUCTION

Living in an Upside-Down Kingdom

Two roads diverged in a wood, and I—I took the one less traveled by, And that has made all the difference. (Robert Frost)

Robert Frost tricked all of us. This poem has been quoted thousands of times and yet we miss the point. The clue to Frost's trickery is found in the letter sent to Leonidas W. Payne Jr. *"My poems—I should suppose everybody's poems—are all set to trip the reader head foremost into the boundless."*[1] The more one thinks about it, the more difficult it is to be sure who is doing what and which way is the right way. The scholar Mark Richardson puts the poem in proper perspective:

"Which road, after all, is the road "not taken"? Is it the one the speaker takes, which, according to his last description of it, is "less traveled"—that is to say, not taken *by others*? Or does the title refer to the supposedly better-traveled road that the speaker himself fails to take? Precisely *who* is *not* doing the taking?"[2]

"The Road Not Taken," is neither an imaginative sonnet nor

a shady trick. It lies somewhere in between. It establishes the traveler's tension created by the decision that must be made. Life is about choices. It cannot be avoided. Speaking of roads and choices, do you choose the broad road or the narrow road? It seems like Jesus said something like that.

What if I told you this book could make your wildest dreams come true? I know, sounds too good to be true, right? What if God created a pathway leading to a heavenly reality? But what if most people don't find that path? Wouldn't that be sad? However, you could be the one making the right choice.

Let's go back to the theme of roads and choices. Jeremiah isn't a poet, but he is a prophet and his words are truer still than those of Mr. Frost. There is no poetic trickery in these words. *"Thus, says the LORD: "Stand by the roads, and look, and ask for the ancient paths, where the good way is; and walk in it, and find rest for your souls. But they said, 'We will not walk in it.'"*

A shocking response. They made the wrong choice. But some will make the right choice. These words from Ellicott's Commentary has a prophetic ring to them. "In the prophet's mind the people were as a traveler who has taken a self-chosen path and finds that it leads him to a place of peril. Is it not well that they should stop and ask where are the old paths, (literally, *the eternal paths*), on which their fathers had safely traveled? Of these old paths they were to choose that which was most distinctly "the good way."³

I hope you choose the ancient path, the good way, for it is the way that leads to joy, peace, and your destiny. Make the right choice. Buck the system. Follow the Holy Spirit. Dreams do come true and your dreams will fulfill Jesus' dreams. His dream for you will give you greater pleasure than you've ever imagined, not only in this life but in your eternal life to come. The prophet's road less traveled will lead you away from the pleasures of this world to a heavenly world filled with incredible possibilities.

Sadly, many do not choose this path, the road less traveled. The other road, the broad way, might seem appealing, but it is fraught with all kinds of danger. On that road, you won't find what you're looking for. The pleasure you seek in this life is not achievable, not through a college degree nor advancing upward into a higher level of socio-economic status. Self-help programs, financial success, notoriety, and all the world might not provide what you really need.

Jesus was the master of asking just the right question at the right time. By one estimate, Jesus asked as many as 307 questions. The question in John 1:38 might be one of the most penetrating questions ever asked, which continues to plague all seekers to this very day. After Jesus returned from the temptation in the wilderness, two followers of John the Baptist began seeking him. After two days of doggedly chasing after him, Jesus turned and asked the question. *Then Jesus turned, and seeing them following, said to them, "What are you looking for?"* How you answer the question determines what you truly desire and where your life is headed. Carefully consider the choice you make. Pick the right way, the narrow way. It might seem to be the hard way, but it is easier than you imagine.

Embracing the crucified life is the only life worth living, and it leads to what you were really looking for, ecstasy, serenity, and reality. I am not saying it will always be easy. There will be times when you might have to walk through the dark night on your way to glory. The good news is that you will not walk alone. You might find that the night is more magnificent and priceless than you could imagine. Consider the poetic words of St. John of the Cross.

> O guiding night!
> O night more lovely than the dawn!
> O night that has united
> the Lover with his beloved,
> transforming the beloved in her Lover.

Come on a journey with me and if you dare, let Jesus' exhalation become your next inhalation. It's time to get lost again!

1

THE ART OF GETTING LOST

Staying vulnerable is a <u>risk</u> we have to take if we want to experience connection.[1]

WHEN YOU ASK SOMEONE WHAT IT MEANS TO BE VULNERABLE, THEY often see it as a synonym for weakness. In some cases, to be vulnerable means to be at risk of experiencing harm or damage. In the military, vulnerability in the face of the enemy is putting yourself in harm's way. If your home is near a river and you fail to buy the flood insurance, you are "vulnerable" to damage to your home without the ability to pay for the repairs. However, being vulnerable means something else when desiring to connect with God and humans.

Dr. Brené Brown, a research professor at the University of Houston, is best-known for her famous TED talk, "The Power of Vulnerability." There is great truth in her well-known statement. "Vulnerability is the birthplace of innovation, creativity, and change."[2]

Bravely, without reluctance, I step into the valley of vulnerability. I won't go into great detail about my past life. I will give you the microwave version of my story. I grew up in a musical family! It seems like most families have a black sheep. I was the outwardly obtuse black sheep of my family. I felt like the horse's tail, always coming in last.

It didn't take long before I dove into the deep end of the pool, and it appears I was comfortable drowning. But I wasn't. I was suffocating in the endless days of my youth. I needed to find God's exhale and hadn't a clue how to find it! So, what did I do?

I chose to escape through Satan's counterfeit of sex (outside of marriage), drugs, and rock n roll. I was a rebel without a cause. Despite the dark path I had chosen, deep inside, I could feel the Spirit wooing me, calling me home.

THE MIRACLE BABY, THE ANGRY CHILD

I had forgotten I was a miracle baby. I should have been aborted because my mom had an IUD hook in her uterus, which was a contraceptive device to kill fertilized eggs. My mom had no idea of the atrocities of the IUD hook. She was very naïve, as most women are who take that route.

It was a miracle I was even born. I had a 1% chance of making it through the device. I didn't know it, but I was living next to a death device! Later in life, at the age of five, my mom pulled me aside and told me the story.

Afterward, she did something strange but wonderful. She told me to close my eyes in prayer and then asked me what I saw in her womb. I responded with something phenomenal. I told her I saw Jesus walking up to her and he had something extraordinarily little in his hand and was giving it to her. The gift was me. He saved me from death because he had a plan for my life and for the lives of many lost souls who would be saved through my ministry.

Growing up in a family of alcoholics, coupled with a boatload of other issues, my anger became my partner in a strange way. Unfortunately, the anger caused me to bypass the will of God for my life. When I was young, like a leech, a demon attempted to attach itself to me and abort my calling in Jesus Christ. I'm happy to say I was set free from alcoholism and the old man was crucified with Christ, and the new man now lives by the power of the son of God. Also, my mom was an alcoholic, but I am so thankful she was set free from a life of addiction to alcohol. I am at peace, knowing my mom is in heaven now.

I was the high school student every mother warned other mothers about. My influence was extremely negative, and I don't blame those moms now. I was a gutter punk in the street's alley, and I was going down for the last count. With one hundred percent certainty, had it not been for God's mercy and the prayers of my family, I would have died long ago and gone to hell on a drug overdose.

However, unbeknownst to me, I was a dark horse evangelist in the making. Years later, when I got saved and became a missionary, it shocked all those moms at the Christian school I attended.

My story is remarkably similar to many people. As I was growing up, the devil tried to destroy my family, as he does with every family, but he lost! I got saved at the age of six. Subsequently, I spent most of my life running from God and did not realize that the most expensive trip is the act of running from

God. At the time, I didn't know you can't outrun God. He is a God who relentlessly pursues the prodigal.

THE DAYS OF RUNNING ENDED

While I was in college, the days of running ended when my parent's prayers intersected with my life at 21. I had an encounter that I would never forget. One night, during a deep sleep, I was shown that I was going to hell. Two weeks later, out of fear of losing my soul, I surrendered my life to Christ. It wasn't until years later that I would fully understand that heavenly word *surrender.* By the way, hell is terrifying, and I am warning you to never go there! Whatever you do in your life, DO NOT MISS HEAVEN! You will regret it eternally.

In spite of my surrender to God and all the mission trips and ministry endeavors, I spent most of my Christian walk defeated. Unfortunately, I still did not understand the elementary principles of walking with God. When I did discover those stunning realities, it changed my life forever. I found an unbelievable ecstasy in God through his Holy Spirit. I encountered unspeakable joy in an unusual place. I found it in the crucified life. *I have been crucified with Christ; it is no longer I who live, but Christ lives in me; and the life which I now live in the flesh I live by faith in the Son of God, who loved me and gave Himself for me* (Gal. 2:20) .

As an angst-filled youth, I got high on drugs, but I thank God that Jesus saved me and showed me a better way of living. If you could multiply, by a million times, the feeling I felt in those days of drug use, would still not equal the pleasure I found in knowing the Holy Spirit. My life was drastically rearranged. I was losing myself in Jesus and radical obedience to His teachings.

HUNGRY FOR GOD

It was their last meeting with Jesus, as the disciples gathered around him. While they were eating together, Jesus left them with these final words. *But ye shall receive power, after that the Holy Ghost is come upon you* (Acts 1:8). Then, it happened. He ascended to heaven and sat down on his throne among the angels worshiping their glorious king.

The disciples returned to Jerusalem. A few days later, they gathered together to celebrate Pentecost. While in prayer, they came under the influence of the Holy Spirit, being filled with the Holy Spirit; it was a moment of holy exhilaration that empowered them to change the world. They did change the world! Gill's Exposition powerfully describes the impact of the Holy Spirit on the little gathering of devoted disciples. The power of the Holy Ghost "strengthened them to preach the Gospel and work miracles in confirmation of it, and courage and greatness of mind, amidst all reproaches and persecutions, to face and oppose their enemies, profess the name of Christ, abide by his truths and ordinances, make their way through all opposition and difficulties, and spread the Gospel all over the world."[3]

This power is the power that changes lives and tramples demons underfoot! It is a dynamite power that floods hearts with astonishment, leads captivated hearts into ecstasies and trances, sets at liberty the most wounded soul, and fortifies the Christian against hell's onslaught and anything he might conjure up or produce against the believer.

This scripture has always been very inviting to me! I first got filled with the Holy Ghost at age 21. I had decided to go into my prayer closet and not come out until God had baptized me with His Holy Ghost fire! I'll never forget it! Do you know what determination got me that experience after waiting for hours? It was refusing to be refused. It was raw hunger!

Blessed are those who hunger and thirst for righteousness, for they will be filled. The Holy Spirit loves to fill desperate vessels! (Matt. 5:6). There was more to face in my walk with God. During those hours, while locked in the closet, I found that one experience wasn't enough. I wanted more of the loving intoxication in the presence of God!

Matthew's words were raw for me, not fully processed yet, but it created flashes of desperate hunger. The expedition began. I'll never forget when I was at a Rodney Howard Browne camp meeting in Tampa, Florida. Those meetings were characterized by people enveloped in holy laughter while spread out all over the place. It seemed that they were experiencing pure bliss. Many people were on the floor giggling, cackling, and laying down in their seats in awe. They were having the time of their lives and I was filled with holy jealousy. They had a touch from God that I didn't, and I wanted it! I had driven to the meetings with some friends. I desperately wanted a touch from God, and I wasn't going to leave without it!

SOAKING IN ECSTASY

It was in that exasperated and hungry state that I saw my friend, Charlie Shamp, shouting from the top of his lungs, "God over here, over here! Over here!" He wanted to get blasted in the Holy

Ghost and he lost his reputation to get it! Oh yes! That reputation thing. I might be hitting a soft spot, but I can promise you it is not worth keeping the golden calf of pride compared to the glory of God!

My reputation is in God's hands. He owns it as much as he owns everything else in my life. Jesus said if any man loses his life, he will find it! *For whoever wishes to save his life will lose it; but whoever loses his life for My sake will find it* (Matt. 16:25). It is a dynamic principle of spiritual life. He who is bent on saving his life will lose it.

You would be surprised how many things we hold on to that stop us from uncontaminated joy, like a roadblock preventing us from finding better things in Papa God. In this case, it was his reputation. *But made Himself of no reputation, taking the form of a bondservant, and coming in the likeness of men* (Phil 2:7). How often do we sacrifice the greater glory realms of God to keep our temporal reputation, respectability, and pride?

I understood this principle and felt that laying down my reputation would be a good thing, even if it meant the ushers would kick me out of the church. So, I began screaming in unison with Charlie. To my surprise, the ushers never came and kicked me out. To my greater surprise, Rodney Howard Browne called me forward, along with all the youth from my church, and prayed for us. We went down to the ground, like anvils falling from the sky.

If we are out of our mind, it is for God; if we are of sound mind, it is for you (2 Cor. 5:13, Berean Study Bible). All I know is that during that moment, it was for God! I was beside myself! I was out of my mind! I remember feeling entirely dizzy in blessed bliss and unspoiled delight. We went out to eat at a restaurant after that service and I felt like I was floating on air. There were 100 million volts of pure ecstasy running through every vein in my body. It felt so good I didn't want anything to break the fellowship with the Lord I was feeling that day. Just trying to pick up my fork to eat my salad seemed like a very distracting experience. I was having a hard time doing it. Even something as simple as looking at freshly paved concrete was wildly interesting and wonderful. There is no high like the Most High, as they said back in the day.

If heaven felt like this, I would not miss it for the world! It was heaven on earth! Suddenly, I realized that if I knew then what I know now, I would never have used drugs or wasted all the money I spent on meaningless things. I just didn't know this feeling was available by my Creator.

JUST ONE TOUCH

I've heard many ministers say just one touch from God, and you will never be the same. That feeling of ecstasy still comes in ebbs and flow. It has never left me since that day, and my life has never been the same! It all started that night when I cried out "Over here! Over here! Right here, God, right now!" at the intense camp meeting.

And what do I see flying like clouds to Israel, like doves to their nests? (Isa 60:68) That was me! I was flying and I never wanted to come down! I got so hungry for that feeling that I went through a period in my life where I stayed that way for days and days. I can remember waking up with that feeling and going to sleep in the same state of exhilaration. I recall lying on the floor for hours in my home, unable to get up and function as a normal human being. God was taking me somewhere, and he didn't want me trying to come down.

Sometimes, it happened when I took my kids to a children's movie and I ended up not having a clue what the plot was because I was gone! The ecstasies would show up when I didn't invite them and even when I wasn't praying. I was not pressing into heaven anymore; heaven was pressing into me.

If someone had come up to me and offered me $100 million to take away that experience for the rest of my life, I would gladly turn them down. The world could have their riches and fame. I just wanted to lift up Jesus' holy name.

My wife, Jennifer, became my designated driver because I could scarcely use my limbs to operate the vehicle. My body and mind felt as if they were dripping in electric honey, jolted by thousands of pleasures, and love coursing through every part of my body. Untold delight, unlimited grace, and unsurpassed intoxication sent me rolling through a season of wonder. Visions would come to me in soaking sessions, and I was wildly intoxicated in the presence of the Holy Spirit, in private and in public. Sometimes, I would be in the middle of working on the financial reports for my accountant and it would hit me while working on the finances. It would hit me during play. It would hit me unannounced, any time of the day. It still happens almost daily.

God bless my darling wife's heart. I remember how many loads of dishes she had to clean, without my help, because I didn't know how to navigate through the sense of euphoria. Since then. I have learned to function under the anointing of ecstasy, but I do not try to hide it from anyone. No matter what it looks like, I let the glory anvils of God fall on my head! I just want that Acts 1:8 Holy Ghost power gushing through my life for the lost. I don't care what it looks like, I love what it feels like, and I just want His Glory, at any cost.

Little did I know that the anointing I was receiving from him would cause a greater release of miracles and signs and wonders in our ministry and that it would catapult us into a soul-winning, full-time ministry. I soaked in him for weeks and months on end while practicing the Presence of the Holy Spirit. It was taking me to a higher place.

GIVEN MUCH, REQUIRED MUCH

I was sought by those who did not ask for Me; I was found by those who did not seek Me. (Isa 65:1) I cannot take any credit for the life I now live. He found me when I was lost. The only thing I could do was submit myself to him and humble myself under the mighty hand of God (I Peter 5:6). What I found to be unique was the more I yielded to the divine ecstasy, the greater his presence would intoxicate me. If I were ever ashamed of how I acted, I would try to sober up in front of people. When I did that, it would lift off. I didn't want that, and I would quickly repent, and the feeling would come back.

It also catapulted me into a realm of the glory of God that introduced me to visions of Christ with dreams and visitations to heaven. It also increased my ability to discern his voice through the word of knowledge and gift of prophecy. I love being filled and filled and filled.

The Spirit of the Lord is upon me, for he has anointed me to bring Good News to the poor. He has sent me to proclaim that captives will be released, that the blind will see, that the oppressed will be set free (Luke 4:18).

The Spirit of the Lord comes upon us for a unique reason. It's not just for our goosebumps; it's to transform lives, eternally. The baptism of the Holy Ghost is a wonderful feeling, but it is also a call to greater surrender! The doors are on the floor. The path to glory goes by way of the cross. While everyone takes the high road, it is the low road that leads to new heights. The way of Jesus contradicts the way of the world. If you are slapped, you offer the other cheek. When you are mocked, you offer blessings in return with a smile on your face. God put a smile on the face of this broken old soul and sent me soaring to heights I never dreamed possible. The more we obey the words of Christ, the greater the joy, and the more we receive, the more we lay down. Conversely, the more we cling to this life, the more we lose.

Ponder the words of Jesus.

From everyone who has been given much, much will be required; and to whom they entrusted much, of him they will ask all the more (Luke 12:48).

If you cling to your life, you will lose it, and if you let your life go, you will save it (Luke 17:33).

These words of Jesus are not the ones you will hear preached in the seeker-sensitive mega-churches. They are the forgotten words, but they cannot be ignored. The narrow road leads to greater levels of that pure bliss. I found massive joy in losing my selfish ambitions of the flesh and trading my desires for the will of God. Though he knew the price to be paid, Jesus humbly said, "Not my will but yours be done." (Luke 22:42) Joy and peace are the rewards of those willing to embrace the cross, as Jesus did.

Behold, I am coming soon, bringing my reward with me, to repay each one for what he has done (Rev. 22:12). I love these words of Jesus. They are encouraging words for those that take the path less chosen. Jesus always rewards the willing heart who becomes a laid-down lover. He rewards us in this life and the one to come. I find that the more radically obedient I become to the words of Christ, the more I find myself lost in the greater pleasures of heaven.

UPSIDE-DOWN KINGDOM

I am finding that this is an upside-down kingdom. Whenever I radically do what my flesh nature opposes, there is a greater reward in the Spirit for me. In fact, its principals are life-altering! Lose your 'old man' and find the upside-down Kingdom of God.

When was the last time you rejoiced and jumped up and down when you got an electric bill and didn't have the money to pay it? It doesn't make sense, does it? To the carnal mind, it doesn't make sense, but it makes sense to the Holy Spirit. In the topsy-turvy, upside-down world of the kingdom, complaining is replaced with thankfulness, fear with peace, judging others with loving others, and frustration with patience. The upside-down kingdom leads you right through the gates of God.

When's the last time your bank account was empty, but you believed God was going to fill it? When was the last time people spoke bad things about you, and you responded by loving them and praying for them? When's the last time you lost yourself while speaking in tongues? You have to lose your mental reasoning because the mind can't understand your prayer language in the Spirit. Speaking in tongues causes an overflow of the Spirit.

My wife and I were able to emerge out of $50,000 debt by giving our way out of it. Subsequently, we almost paid our full mortgage, and we were able to invest in mutual funds, and we created college savings for our kids. It all came by giving our way into Father's riches.

I have found some of my favorite people to love are the ones who treated me the worst. I had to lose my sense of vengeance. Once I loved them, it was my gift back to God for all he forgave me for!

I have found greatness in ministry by serving. I lost my sense of greatness and traded it for God's sense of greatness. The words of Jesus contradict the philosophies of this world. The greatest of all is the servant of all. The more you lose your life, the more you find your life in God. Never grow tired of hearing the radical, magnificent, counter-cultural good news of Jesus!

"Yes," Jesus replied, "and I assure you that everyone who has given up house or brothers or sisters or mother or father or children or property, for my sake and the Good News, will receive now in return a hundred times as many houses, brothers, sisters, mothers, children, and property—along with persecution. And in the world to come, that person will have eternal life."

In fact, I have found that my favorite state, being intoxicated in the Holy Spirit, often comes because I go out and give him away to the lost as I preach the gospel to them, and a hundred-fold return in perfect delight!

I found that there is more rest when I go out every single day and love on the lost souls. It is greater than spending every day resting and binge-watching Netflix after a hard day of work. Don't get me started there.

Taking time to lose my life to disciple a new young believer has sometimes caused my life to rub off on them. I like the fact that some of the people I discipled are outrunning me in ministry. There is joy in finding the doors are on the floor!

I am telling you that all of Heaven wants to hijack you and take you on a flight so high you never imagined the limitless possibilities. These opportunities come your way as you daily demonstrate the fruits of the Spirit!

Recently, I crossed over 350 days of evangelism, and I am the happiest man on planet earth. I have more love in my heart for Jesus than I've ever had in 19 years of ministry and more joy and more peace than I've ever had. It's all because I'm losing myself in Him.

I've had Muslims tell me Jesus feels incredible after we prayed with them. Finding Jesus is life-changing, as my lost friends discover when they give their hearts to him. I've had the privilege of watching God heal the cripple. People get new teeth and other amazing creative miracles, like watching years of crippling disease and pains healed to the Glory of God. It is all made possible when I lose my selfish pride in Jesus and become like a child.

Consider this question, and I know you have asked it. What if nothing happens when I pray for the sick, what if they don't get healed? This is what happened to me. I let go of the doubt because I found the miracles come through faith.

Everything I have shared with you is available for you right now. What are you willing to do to receive it? Are you willing to do what seems hard, maybe even impossible? It's not complicated. It is quite simple. Listen to the words of Jesus and obey him. Living my life in obedience to Christ is the easiest and most enjoyable life I have ever known.

Did you know how sweet Jesus is and that he won't even break a bruised reed? He deeply cares for you, and he wants you to salivate over his blessings. Jesus' words are music for the ear. *My yoke is easy and my burden is light* (Matt. 11:30).

It's time for heaven to hijack you. Are you ready for it? Eternal bliss can begin now. Good, I am glad you are! Let's get on with it then.

2

FIRST ADAM, LAST ADAM

Millenniums in a moment. A million miles in a step. An ocean in a drop. Volumes in a word. A race in a woman. A hell of suffering in an act. The depths of woe in a glance. The first chapter of Romans in Genesis three, six. Sharpest pain in softest touch. God mistrusted-distrusted. Satan embraced. Sin's door open. Eden's gate shut. [1]

THE TRANSFORMATION FROM THE RANCID OLD MAN TO THE restored new man is a mind-blowing euphoric celebration of life in Christ. Losing the old man and embracing the new man, in Christ, is the beginning of something wonderful. First, we need to go back in time before we move forward.

In the beginning, there was only one will, the will of Father and all creation lived in harmony under this solitary rule, heaven's rule. The rebellious act of man introduced another will, the will of the flesh. Adam supplanted Father's will, causing chaos as it extended through time and space. An eerie echo reverberated throughout the created world. "Man was now separated from

God. Lusting after the earthly, the holy anointing oil, given of Christ, was dried up; he became shut up in a bestial image."[2]

Critically wounded by the injection of the 'self' virus, man became spiritually disabled. C.S. Lewis said it well when he said he felt like a man brought out under naked heaven, on the edge of a precipice, into the teeth of a wind that came from the Pole.

> Then came, at a predetermined moment, a moment in
> time and of time,
> A moment not out of time, but in time, in what we call
> history: transecting, bisecting the world of time, a
> moment in time but not like a moment of time,
> A moment in time but time was made through that
> moment for without the meaning there is no time, and
> that moment of time gave the meaning.[3]

When the time was right, perfectly positioned at the right moment, Jesus descended into our world, stripping himself of all heavenly advantages. He who created the world will now save the world. He is the word who now speaks the word.

With the background sound of crackling concrete, men began to feel a life pushing upward out of the hardness of the old man as they listened to the words of Jesus. Never had they experienced such joy and acceptance like they felt in his presence. More was to come. The new life is made possible by the second Adam.

> For as in Adam all die, so also in Christ shall all be made alive
> (I Cor. 15:22).

And so it is written, The first man Adam was made a living soul; the last Adam was made a quickening spirit (I Cor. 15:45).

Just as we have borne the image of the earthy, we will also bear the image of the Heavenly (1 Cor. 15:49).

LOSING OURSELVES IN JESUS

For years, the Lord has been showing me the truth of who we are in Jesus and what it means to be losing ourselves in him. Unfortunately, it took me many painful years to learn how to fully surrender to what was revealed. I sense what some call warfare or spiritual attacks are simply the consequences of submitting to our fleshly nature. We need our souls cleansed from the lingering repercussions of the old man. First, we must fully appreciate and apprehend our new identity in Jesus, putting his words into practice every minute. Paul's words are so clear.

If any man be in Christ, he is a new creature: old things are passed away; behold, all things are become new (2 Cor. 5:17).

Do not lie to one another, since you laid aside the old self with its evil practices, and have put on the new self who is being renewed to a true knowledge according to the image of the One who created him (Eph. 4:22).

'Loose' it is the common reoccurring theme in this book. Do not rush; consider these verses.

[Is] not this the fast that I have chosen? to loose the bands of wickedness, to undo the heavy burdens, and to let the oppressed go free, and that ye break every yoke? (Isa 58:6)

And when Jesus saw her, he called [her to him], and said unto her, Woman, thou art loosed from thine infirmity. (Luke 13:12)

And he that was dead came forth, bound hand and foot with graveclothes: and his face was bound about with a napkin. Jesus saith unto them, Loose him, and let him go. (John 11:44)

Problematically, many recognize losing the old man is a great victory, but I am not sure if they get the big picture. They rejoice in the fact that they once had a perverted spirit, but now, they are clean, but they fail to recognize that holding on to unbelief is just as perverse and sinful. We celebrate victories over addictions, gambling, or things like fornication, but we fail to repent from things that are displeasing to the Lord, like anger or gossiping. We blame anger on our old Irish or German tempers, claiming that we are all human, and it surfaces frequently! Blame shifting is also a sign of the old man.

But we are not human anymore! We are the new man, and our life is hidden in Christ. By now, you should have lost your anger problem because you are in Christ. Jesus said that if we are angry with our brother, we are in danger of hellfire. *But I say unto you, That whosoever is angry with his brother without a cause shall be in danger of the judgment: and whosoever shall say to his brother, Raca, shall be in danger of the council: but whosoever shall say, Thou fool, shall be in danger of hell fire* (Matt. 5:22). Over 2000 years ago, all our sins were nailed to the cross through the sacri-

fice of Jesus. We must lose that old man realizing that it is not our identity anymore. With desire and desperation, daily put on Christ!

Many are in financial bondage because they have an Ebenezer Scrooge heart and won't let go. *Give, and it will be given to you: good measure, pressed down, shaken together, and running over will be put into your bosom. For with the same measure that you use, it will be measured back to you* (Luke 6:38). A kind and generous man to the poor and helpless demonstrates the character of a generous heart. According to the measure you give, you will receive. Great are the riches that belong to a generous soul. On the other hand, the one who is stingy and closed hearted will find few, if any, who will aid him when he is in need.

The way of the miser is not how to build a prosperous business. They are willing to venture into uncharted territory. No risk, no reward. Another thing to remember, we are not bound to a tithe. I heard one person put it this way. In the Old Testament, we are taught how much to give, but in the New Testament, we ask Jesus how much we should keep. My wife and I saw our finances perform a total 180, from debt to abundance. We attribute the dramatic change to abandoning our stingy spirits, long ago, and we give all to the glory of God. Literally, we gave our way out of debt and it was incredible watching God's miracles taking place right before our eyes.

CHURCH ARISING

People are starving to know who they are in Christ. When we become followers of Jesus, we lose our identity in this world and embrace our identity in Christ. Amid the many voices in our heads that wage war against our identity, we forget who we are in Christ. Watchman Nee got it right when he said, "Outside of Christ, I am weak; Inside of Christ I am strong."[4] John R.W. Stott wrote a remarkable article for the C.S. Lewis Institute, entitled *In Christ: The Meaning and Implications of the Gospel of Jesus Christ*. Here is a small portion of that article. "The commonest description in the Scriptures of a follower of Jesus is that he or she is a person "in Christ." The expressions "in Christ," "in the Lord," and "in him" occur 164 times in the letters of Paul alone, and are indispensable to an understanding of the New Testament. To be "in Christ" does not mean to be inside Christ, as tools are in a box or our clothes in a closet, but to be organically united to Christ, as a limb is in the body or a branch is in the tree. It is this personal relationship with Christ that is the distinctive mark of his authentic followers."[5]

God is preparing the church to stand center stage in world transformation! The body of Christ, as it embraces the fullness of the gospel of Jesus, will become the most creative force known to mankind and recognized throughout the universe. There is a remnant in the church that arises during this hour, as they recover the truth of what our salvation was truly intended to be. What would it be like if you were like the Apostle Peter? Imagine if it were dangerous for anyone to be touched by your shadow, and they were healed or blessed by it.

Get ready to be awakened to the endless possibilities inside you, made possible by the Christ within. As carriers of the joy of Jesus, you are called to be part of a magnificent remnant army that is ready to invade the earth with God's blessings,

The remnant in the church I am talking about will be the catalysts for the greatest outpouring the earth has ever known.

How you ask? The church is the key. However, it is time to stop playing church and start being the church. But how will we be the church unless we know what the church was meant to be?

The church cannot be accurately defined until we grasp the regal call on our lives. The Greek word for church is "ecclesia" and means "the called-out ones." It also carries the meaning of ambassadors, senators, and judiciaries! To build upon this, put into perspective the Bible translation of Paul's day, the Septuagint. "This is how it is rendered in Deuteronomy 4:10 ("assemble the people before me") using the word *ekklēsia* — the gathering together of the Lord's people as a covenant community before their covenant God."[6]

KINGDOM EXPLODING

And there are also many other things that Jesus did, which if they were written one by one, I suppose that even the world itself could not contain the books that would be written (John 21:25). The ministry of Jesus was a combination of miracles and teaching. With astonishing, captivating stories and illustrations, Jesus taught the crowds the ways of God and summoned them to live according to those ways. Jesus had compassion for the disenfranchised and disheartened. He dramatically expressed his compassion and proved his authority with miracles.

The parables of Jesus make up a central and critical part of the teachings of Jesus. Through the capability of his wisdom, he helped the common people understand deep spiritual truths by telling a story, stories we call parables. Jesus told seven short, pithy parables of the kingdom, enabling the people to understand the reality of the kingdom. The kingdom parables included the parables of the sower and the seed, the tares, the mustard seed, the leaven, the pearl of great price, the dragnet, and the hidden treasure.

Three of the kingdom parables illustrate the wealth and joy of discovering the kingdom. *The Kingdom of Heaven is like a man who found treasure in a field, and with joy he hid the treasure again, and went and sold all he had to buy the field* (Matthew 13:44).

The *unexpected* discovery, the consequent excitement and joy, and the eagerness to buy at any sacrifice are the keys to be observed in the interpretation. The point of the parable lies in the man's "earnestness," his anxiety, his care, and obtaining it. It is hidden from most people. When a person sees it and hears it, he must sacrifice all that hinders his obtaining it, and to seek it with the earnestness with which other people seek for gold. Alfred Barnes colorfully describes the center of reality in Jesus' story. "The truth often lies buried: it is like rich veins of ore in the sacred Scriptures; it must be searched out with diligence, and its discovery will repay a man for all his sacrifices."[7]

We are ambassadors of the greatest Kingdom that ever was and ever will be. When we discover the kingdom, it is our ambition to live our life in unison with the principles of the kingdom of God. It took me a while to realize that I was part of royalty, a kingdom dignity. As the truth dawned upon me, I humbly accepted that it IS God's will to manifest this delegated authority in the earth, by his grace through Jesus Christ. It is not just His will for my life, but also every believer in the body of Christ.

We have made an imminent and powerful exchange on the trading floor of heaven. We traded our old meaningless way of living and found a new life in Jesus Christ, the King of the Kingdom. This is a world changer!

Rather, clothe yourselves with the Lord Jesus Christ, and do not think about how to gratify the desires of the flesh (Romans 13:14). Through believing in Christ's accomplishment on the cross, and his death, burial, and resurrection, we have been given the advantage no other religion can offer, despite their laborious works. We have exchanged the temporal for the eternal. We have traded mortality for immortality. We have substituted depression for unlimited joy, and hatred for unconstrained love. Believe it or not, we have replaced poverty, shame, and hopelessness for boundless blessings, grace, and power to live by.

We serve a good King and belong to a Kingdom whose government will never cease to increase! Do you want more good news? We all get to share in the glory of God's kingdom and be partakers of it. *Giving thanks unto the Father, which hath made us meet to be partakers of the inheritance of the saints in light* (Col. 12). For *of His fullness we have all received, and grace upon grace* (John 1:16). We are partakers of his fullness, fighting the good fight of faith, not the depressing fight of faith!

LET NO ONE STEAL YOUR JOY

Sadly, the yeast of modern-day Pharisees has crept into the church, tempting many and making many live beneath their divine rights, as sons and daughters of the King. Wrong concepts of Christian eschatology have tempted many to believe that they will be defeated by the darkness of demonic powers, and depraved by the lusts of the flesh, thus robbing them of any chivalry of the soul. They are convinced that Jesus will have to rescue the helpless souls from the earth. The truth is that Christ has already delivered us and *rescued us from the domain of dark-*

ness and translated us to the Kingdom of His beloved Son (Colossians 1:13). Don't get me wrong. Heaven will be great, even better in our new glorified bodies.

There was a moment when I had an incredible dream. I was walking down a path, and I walked into the great wedding procession. The bride of Christ was about to meet her bridegroom. We were so excited that we would soon meet Jesus. We were almost ready to tear ourselves to pieces, overwhelmed with laughter and joy. We know that joy will last forever. It will not be taken away. It was an inward joy in my Spirit, a joy beyond comparison to anything I have ever felt. Here's the good news. We do not have to wait for that jubilant joy. We can have continuous glimpses and experiences of the same joy here on earth.

However, for centuries, false belief systems have invaded the church, attempting to dilute the power of God with unbelief and fear, relegating the power of God's joy to some contaminated ideology, poisoned by false thinking.

This has caused many to forfeit their dreams into the hands of other powerful charismatic spiritual leaders with their miracle ministries. There are too many who don't know they have the same Holy Spirit and can operate in the miraculous. Don't stop dreaming. Allow your imagination to take you to places you never thought possible. Step out of the natural realm that is locked in time and move into the eternal realm, where space and time do not have merits. Eternal life is not some wonderful endowment only to be enjoyed in the great by and by. It is also meant for the here and now. It is to be furiously enjoyed now, as Jesus clearly declared in the gospels

'*This is eternal life that they may know you the only true God and Jesus Christ who you have sent*" (John 17:3). We are NOW eternal beings! We are loved and pursued relentlessly by an eternal God who is love himself.

Outside of time, there is a realm called the Glory realm where all things are possible. It flows from heaven, it flows from within us, and it engulfs us in our praise. We are not of this world. Man is constituted of a different nature and lives in another realm. Darkness cannot win against it, and light will always prevail in this realm, but only when tested and practiced in our daily lives.

Do you know that God knew us before we were fashioned in our mother's wombs? *Before I formed you in the womb, I knew you; Before you were born I sanctified you* (Jeremiah 1:5). The Eternal one is lavishly in love with you. He even had a book about our future before we could live it. It should prove how valuable we are to him. The church recognizes this value, the significance of possessing the potential of metamorphosizing overnight into overcomers. If the world knew this, they would run to the church, seeking the answers and transformation we have discovered in Jesus. We only have as much influence over culture as they see value in us. So, the first step is to realize just how valued we are to Jesus. I am so glad you picked up this book!

My frame was not hidden from You when I was being formed in secret [and] intricately and curiously wrought [as if embroidered with various colors] in the depths of the earth [a region of darkness and mystery]. Your eyes saw my unformed substance, and in Your book all the days [of my life] were written before ever they took shape, when as yet there was none of them. How precious and weighty also are Your thoughts to me, O God! How vast is the sum of them! If I could count them, they would be more in number than the sand. When I awoke, [could I count to the end] I would still be with You (Psalms 139:15-18 Amplified Version).

His love has no limits. To put it like one of my favorite worship leaders of all time put it, "There is no danger in excess of loving Him." (Kevin Prosch) I believe with all my heart that if we become like little children and daily test ourselves and the limitations we have put on God and ourselves, we will find ourselves still breaking barriers we thought were not there.

However, there comes a point when you have to get out of the desert mentality, and breakthrough into the glory realm where, though there may be trials, you will always triumph through Christ in every situation. The false belief systems that held you back yesterday will be passé (Out of date, unfashionable)! Time to take on a whole new wardrobe, and that is your new creation reality. Lose the old man for goodness sake! Do it right now in Jesus' name and enjoy everything that flows from the vine of Jesus Christ. *I am the vine, ye are the branches: He that abideth in me, and I in him, the same bringeth forth much fruit: for without me ye can do nothing* (John 15:5). Lose your insecurity and tell yourself you are a child of the Lord God Jehovah Almighty!

Live upside down for God today and flip the tables on the devil. Radically obey the words of Christ and watch yourself feel reborn again with more angelic hope you could have ever possibly imagined.

3

LOSE MY UNBELIEF, FIND GREATER FAITH

So then faith comes by hearing, and hearing by the word of God"
(Rom. 10:17). Notice it does not say, faith comes from having heard.
The whole nature of faith implies a relationship with God that is
current. The emphasis is on hearing...in the now! (Bill Johnson)[1]

I'LL NEVER FORGET THE TIME I WAS IN ENGLAND, ON THE
streets ministering to those around me. One of the kids on the
street asked if I could make him grow taller. Yes, you are reading
it right. Someone asked me if I could make them grow. The kid
was short and wanted to be bigger. This was a moment in my life
when I had to *lose my unbelief to find great faith in God.*

In Mark 9, there is a story about a lad, afflicted with a
demonic spirit. The son's father brought him to the disciples of
Jesus, hoping his son would be delivered. Unfortunately, they
could not help him. Eventually, the father made his way to Jesus
and explained the horrible condition of his son, ending the story

with a request to heal him. Jesus responded with these classic words repeated many times over the years. *If thou canst believe, all things are possible to him that believeth.* Jesus wanted the father to understand the challenge created by the son's situation. It was not a lack of power; it was a lack of faith. Unbelief sees more in the things that hinder than in God's promise to heal. God can bring the power if you can bring the faith. He will handle the 'doing' if you handle the 'believing.' Do you get Jesus' point?

Causing people to grow, fits in the 'greater work' that Jesus promised. *Most assuredly, I say to you, he who believes in Me, the works that I do he will do also; and greater works than these he will do, because I go to My Father* (John 14:12). Yes, it is all about losing our unbelief, so we can find faith.

A VOYAGE INTO THE MIRACULOUS

The inspiring story started when I was on a mission trip to England. We were invited to teach the conference attendees how to spread the gospel through miracles and words from the Holy Spirit.

Now, it's one thing to go out and distribute gospel tracks to people, which is wonderful, and we do it. Still, it's another thing to take evangelism to a higher level by walking the streets, introducing people to the power of the Holy Spirit, and demonstrating the miraculous. One is easier and the other takes more risk and you can probably guess which one requires greater risks.

Referring to those inducted into the Faith Hall of Fame, Hebrews 11:38 says that the world was not worthy of them. While

I am on this earth, I have always wanted to exchange the worldly for the heavenly. I want the world to not be worthy of me, in Jesus' name! Jesus deserves, and desires that I live that kind of life. He died on the cross for me. Certainly, I can live my life in honor of all he has done for me. We want to see his kingdom come to earth as it is in heaven and hoping people don't give up, in the meantime. Bill Johnson declares that the kingdom of God must never be reduced to talk, ideas, and principles. The kingdom of God is power.

While writing about England, one can't help but remember the greatest evangelist in British history. It is John Wesley, founder of the Methodist church. The classic words of John Wesley come to mind. "Give me one hundred men who love only God with all their heart and hate only sin with all their heart and we will shake the gates of hell and bring in the kingdom of God in one generation."[2] I believe God is raising a new generation of men like John Wesley.

While on the streets, we had a wonderful day in Norwich, England. I believed for great miracles to happen. The last time we were in England we prayed for a woman on the streets who had tumors all over her neck and she was astonished when healed. The tumors disappeared when we prayed for her after interpreting one of her dreams.

We had an incredible day, watching many people walking with a cane who were healed by the power of God, and no longer needed their canes, to the praise of Jesus. On another occasion, we met a group of skateboarders, and to our amazement, we experienced an open heaven. We approached them and I asked one of the kids if they would like to appear on my

YouTube show. They agreed. I asked them if they ever saw anything supernatural. Like you would expect from a group of kids, they responded with several funny answers.

Pressing on, I asked them if anyone had nagging physical symptoms they wanted to disappear. One kid said that he had pain in his back and another kid said he had pain in his hand. I told them to watch God because he is going to do a miracle. Reluctantly, they allowed us to pray for them. While we were praying, every one of them felt the fire of God touch the afflicted part of their body. They were shocked when they were all healed. One kid was mesmerized and spoke out, "Mate I'm dead serious. I feel something touching my back!"

In the course of excitement, God gave me a creative idea. I asked all the kids if they wanted to feel the fire of God, in what I dubbed a fire circle. After they all agreed, we held hands in a circle, and I released the fire of God. They were blown away as they experienced the fire of God on their bodies.

CAN YOU MAKE ME GROW?

By the end of our time with them, one young man's faith had escalated to a crescendo. He told me he took medication for attention deficit disorder that stunted his growth. So, what would be the solution? It was at this point that I was confronted with his question, mentioned at the beginning of this chapter. "Can you make me grow?"

I had to lose something worthless to find something greater. My unbelief had to go! I was immediately tempted to say, "I'm not sure" "I don't know." However, I realized it was foolish pride talking. I knew that with God, all things are possible. The answer to his question blurted out of my mouth. "YES!" By the power of the Holy Spirit, I knew God could make him grow, through the gift of faith, given by the Spirit.

In the stories of Jesus, every single person who asked Jesus for healing was never turned away. He wouldn't say, "Well, I can try" "We'll see what God will do." The Holy Spirit wants us to say 'yes' to people in need!

But when the multitudes knew it, they followed Him; and He received them and spoke to them about the kingdom of God and healed those who had need of healing (Luke 9:11).

While he was saying this, a synagogue leader came and knelt before him and said, "My daughter has just died. But come and put your hand on her, and she will live." Jesus got up and went with him, and so did his disciples. But when the crowd was put outside, He went in and took her by the hand, and the girl arose (Matthew 9:18, 19, 25).

The boy didn't need to think about it; he just knew God would work through him. As I put my hands over his head, I began commanding, in the name of Jesus, to grow, as he had asked me. To everyone's amazement, he began to grow. My cameraman noticed that he grew above the horizon behind him. The team watched the boy grow! Shocked by the miracle, their hearts began to open. The awe of the Spirit filled so many hearts on that day.

You can't please everybody. Amidst those glorious events,

some haters joined us. Suddenly, a group of rude boys came up to us. They began shouting very loudly at the skateboarders. They told them not to listen to us. They accused us of practicing voodoo and trying to sell them something. Sadly, a miracle caused them to assume it's magic! Why can't Jesus get the fame He deserves? I recall where Jesus drove a legion of demons out of a man, and they all ran into a herd of pigs and he was accused of being a magician. (Luke 8:26-39)

I shouldn't be surprised by the kid's responses. It reminds me of the words of Jesus. *A disciple is not above his teacher, nor a servant above his master* (Matthew 10:25). Jesus was opposed and harassed, should we expect anything less?

I could not resist the moment. It was not the time to act like Mr. Nice Guy. If I had, humbly, told them that Jesus loved them, nothing would have happened. I wasn't going down that road. So, I put on my Mr. Warrior cloak preparing myself to challenge them. I stared them in their eyes and responded to their cynicism with these words. "There is more power in my little pinky than all the anti-Christs of hell. All of you come to see me and if I don't hear from God for you, then beat me up, right here on this street.

Talk about putting your neck on the line! Sure enough, the leader of that group of guys came forward. The Holy Spirit gave me a word of knowledge that was accurate for him, a word that revealed his unbelief. I prophesied over him, telling him that he was going to lead many drug addicts to the Lord.

> But if all prophesy, and an unbeliever or outsider enters, he is
> convicted by all, he is called to account by all, and the secrets
> of his heart are disclosed, and so, falling on his face, he will

worship God and declare that God is really among you (I Corinthians 14: 12-13).

Dumbfounded, he wondered how I could have known this, He confessed he was a drug dealer, though he attended church with his family. He knew he wasn't living right for God. He thought it was amazing that I was able to hear the voice of God for him. He was sure God was among us. On the spot, he changed his mind. He did not believe that we were practicing voodoo and knew that the Holy Spirit had sent us, just for him.

As a result, he and his friends got saved, as did the skateboarder kids! My point in telling you the story is there's a way that seems right to a man but, in the end, is death. What might seem right is not always right. If I hadn't put on my Bold suit, I wouldn't have led those kids to Jesus, which would have been death for them. At that moment, I could've said no, but I chose to say yes to God. I believed God could cause him to grow. Being the nice guy, I am, it would have been easy to be kind and polite with the rude boys, thus preventing them from salvation and Christ flowing into their lives. It wouldn't have been good, and I wasn't about to let the devil have his way!

RADICAL BULLDOG FAITH

I had to lose myself that day and discover that all my ideas are not always good. What was better was to be clothed in Christ and talk to them like a warrior, knowing that God would back me up! And on that day, He did!

I have been in services where I had to lose my reputation when I outrageously pressed into God with great risk. I've been in many services where the Lord wanted to give people dental miracles. I humbled myself and asked everyone that wanted a dental miracle to open their mouth because the Bible says open your mouth and I will fill it with good things (Psalm 81:10).

I often asked those that opened their mouth for healing, to have seven people look inside their mouth with flashlights and see if God healed them by putting in a new filling or new tooth or a new gold crown in their mouth. On another occasion, in a meeting, a woman received a new tooth in the space where their teeth were pulled. Others received new shiny gold crowns on teeth that needed work. I have seen it with my own eyes, and it is a sight to behold.

I'll never forget one girl who received a gold tooth in our meeting in Seattle. She went back to her dentist for a checkup. Her dentist curiously asked her where she got the wonderful crown work done. She replied, "What crown work?" God had given her a beautiful shiny new gold crown, without knowing it. The miracle took her family by surprise and the backsliding people in their family gave their life back to Jesus Christ.

I've been in services when the Holy Spirit asked me to tickle someone's legs, to see their shorter leg grow to the same length. Whenever I did something out of the normal, God would show up with his power. You know what? I am not the only guy that does strange things. If Jesus does, so can I.

When He had said these things, He spat on the ground and made clay with the saliva; and He anointed the eyes of the blind man with the clay. And He said to him, "Go, wash in the pool of Siloam" (which is translated, Sent). So, he went and washed, and came back seeing (John 9:6, 7). The Bible says without faith it is impossible to please God (Hebrews 11:6). Why would we operate in any other way?

Speaking of bizarre miracles, the Holy Spirit told someone to buy our ministry a metal detector. Then they prophesied over us that we would bring it to meetings, and God would disintegrate the surgically implanted metal in people's bodies.

I'll never forget that time when I was going to preach at Jeff Jansen's church. Before I left for the meeting, I went to my pantry to look for some food, and I saw the metal detector sitting there. God told me to bring it that night. When the meeting started, I called for people who had metal implants in their bodies to come forward. When we scanned their bodies, the metal detector went off. At that point, we asked the church to decree, in the name of Jesus, for the metal to dissolve. Afterward, we checked the parts of the body where the metal detector found the metal, and we discovered that the metal in their bodies had disappeared!

The only thing I can say is God loves radical bulldog faith. Faith is power, demonstrated when God created the universe by the word and healing miracles through faith. There is creative power in the spoken word because faith is the substance of things hoped for and the evidence of things not seen. There is creative evidence, even before a miracle is manifest (Hebrews 11:1).

It was an amazing thing to meet someone who had stage four cancer and then declare that they are going to live and not die and watch them be healed immediately. If we will steward our faith well and continue to live a lifestyle of fasting and prayer, I believe we will see miracles we've never seen before.

I'll never forget the story a girl told me about what happened while she was soaking in God's presence in one of our meetings while lying on the chairs. She said she doesn't know how but her physical body, seemingly, melted into the chairs and she ended up on the floor, underneath the chairs. She said she experienced what she believes was similar to the time Jesus walked through a wall. She went through the chairs by the power and presence of God.

I saw the Lord raise a woman from the dead on the streets after asking me to pray for her. This amazing miracle happened in my early 20s. I was on my way to visit my folks. As I pulled into my parents neighborhood, I saw a woman laying down on a stretcher with paramedics nearby. After meeting the husband and asking him what happened, he told me she died of a heart attack. After being informed of this, I told him God would raise his wife from the dead. He told me he lost his first wife to a heart attack, so now I knew this was demonic. I stretched my hands towards the woman as they were trying to resuscitate her back to life. They eventually gave up and were about to leave, when all of a sudden, during my praying, she came back to life! She breathed again, after being gone for enough time to give up hope. The paramedics were puzzled and astonished. The reason that God gave me faith for this miracle, was that I had a word of knowledge before I came onto the scene. My chest began to hurt minutes before I even knew what was coming, which wasn't indicating a problem within me, but a word of knowledge for the situation forthcoming. God is so amazing and to Him be all the Glory! Although I've only seen it once, I believe I am just getting started. We are going to pray for the dead, and they are going to awaken, in the name of Jesus Christ!

I believe God the father wants to blow his children's minds

and take them on an incredible joy ride so that we will always thirst and have a desire for more of the miraculous.

P.S. You, the reader, will love this! I recently spoke to the person who was filming the miracle of the kid who asked to grow. He told me he saw the young man recently and he was very tall! Isn't God so amazing?"

4

DISMISSING THE TEMPORAL, EMBRACING THE ETERNAL

To see a world in a grain of sand and heaven in a wildflower. Hold infinity in the palm of your hand and eternity in an hour. (William Blake)

FINDING YOUR ETERNITY IN EACH MOMENT WHILE LIVING IN infinity's sunrise is worth more than the world can offer. Connected between the everyday reality we experience and the infinite landscapes of interstellar beauty, the presence of angels, heavenly glory, and the king sitting on his throne, that feel so close, makes us realize we live between two worlds.

He has made everything beautiful in its time. Also, he has put eternity into man's heart, yet so that he cannot find out what God has done from the beginning to the end (Ecclesiastes 3:11). Some are happy to be immersed in time, but we live in a light that shines high above the roaring sea of circumstances, in which we float like fallen leaves upon the water.

When I was a young child, I knew no boundaries in my mind. The borders of my imagination extended as far as my mind would take me, as long as I chose not to put restrictions on my thoughts. At the age of five, I can recall being able to comprehend eternity. The Lord would allow my contemplation to take me into the depth of mystery. There were times in my youth while lying on my bed at night, I felt like I was traveling at an amazing speed. At that point in my life, my mind could only grasp the length and expanse of eternity, though I could remember my spirit taking over and revealing to me the feeling of endlessness. Sometimes, I still remember traveling in my imagination so far into the future that eternity would begin to scare me. It wasn't fear in a negative sense; it was more like overwhelming awe and beautiful dread of God's resplendent glory and magnanimous nature. It would thrill my soul to ponder how He always has been, and He always will be. I wondered if my spirit remembered, outside of time, before I was created, knowing that outside of time, in the glory realm of God where there is no end nor beginning.

Growing up in church and hearing about heaven and hell, there were times when I would try to imagine eternity in both realms. When I went deep in a meditation about eternity and thinking about being in Heaven, forever with the Prince of Peace, great joy and peace would flood my soul. It made me happy to embrace and love life on earth, though it was hard to fathom that it will never cease to exist, it seemed like the greatest gift God could give mankind!

ETERNITY IS A LONG TIME

Great sorrow and grief-filled my soul when, at times, I felt juxta-posed between the beautiful reality that I experienced in the deep mediation of eternity and, on the other side, what it must be like for those, separated from Jesus and perishing without knowing this glorious salvation that is an undeserved gift for all mankind. It would fill my heart with the burden for those who do not know Christ or those who live in unrepented, hidden, and intentional sin.

I cannot tell a lie; I liked thinking of endlessness with Jesus far more! To imagine life and to continue into perfect bliss, for eons and eons, was an addiction for me as a child. That is why it is sad to watch so many choosing to believe there is no life after death. Simply ceasing to exist, how could they accept that? What they don't realize is that death has already been defeated at the cross. God is eternal and we are made in His image and we were not created to die. We will spend eternity with Jesus, either in heaven or away from him in hell.

Seriously, why would anyone want life to stop, entering into a void of nothingness? Even when I was lost in sin and diag-nosed with clinical depression at 16, I did not want to stop living. Something inside me wanted to keep reaching forward. At least, some can do better and believe in reincarnation. I am not endorsing that belief because it is false. But, at least, it shows the spirit inside many people DO want to keep living!

Back to the atheists, many of them believe that when they breathe their last breath, life will end, and they will cease to exist. When I was a teenager, I pondered what life after death might be like. I concluded that, if there was no afterlife, the point of living had no point. It would be a hilarious parody. No painter in their right mind spends months creating an exquisite work of art and burns it up when completed. It would contradict logic, on all ends. If anyone says they don't believe in life after death, they are lying to you. They have chosen deception because eternity is in every man's heart. (Ecclesiastes 3:11) This belief system is a direct diversion from a beautiful thing called surrender. It is a flawed attempt at disengaging from serving the one true God.

GET THE POWER BACK!

I'm under the impression that more than half the church has done an incredible job of misrepresenting Jesus in all his sublime beauty. It is no wonder myriads of people, in so-called Christian nations, have run to agnosticism, new age, or other substitutes. Let's look at the occult, for example. Many run to the occult, thinking it is a scientific alternative to the narrow mindedness they have seen in the church. In reality, however, the occult is just a flawed attempt by fallen demons' efforts to mimic or copy the glory of God.

It is time the church recovers the treasure in their field (Matthew 13:44). Discovering the great treasure within, the world would run to the church, seeking the goodness, light, love, and mercy that will, effortlessly, ooze out of them like honey, horizon upon the horizon. A sweet-toothed world wants the ultimate sugary truth and enthusiastically desires to experience the supernatural!

It's time for the church to get the power back. Amaze and daze the new age community with the power of God and win them to Christ. I don't believe the Christian nations must backslide. But if they do, I believe we can help win them back to Jesus.

How ironic! What has happened to the imaginations of those in the body of Christ? If just one percent of the body of Christ in the world would not allow the restrictions of the doubt to put a blockade in between them and what God wants to accomplish through them, I believe the whole world would be turned upside down, as it happened in the book of Acts. Educational systems and manmade scientific philosophies demystify the wonder of creation and have incapacitated people's perceptions. This exposes them to the crippling disease of doubt and life limited by mere meager possibilities.

WAKE UP SLEEPING BEAUTY

It is no wonder that so many people in our world are starving for the supernatural and extraordinary. Who can blame them? God doesn't blame them at all, in fact, He is head over heels in love with them, waiting for the sleeping beauty, his bride, to wake up and inject the truth of his word into their spirit man so they can believe and live and not die! I call this a lifestyle evangelism, manifesting Christ to the world through how we live the supernatural life. Steve Sjogren calls it a conspiracy of kindness and love. Your life is your witness. You have no excuse for not giving it a try. In John 14:21, Jesus said, *"He that has my commandments, and keeps them, he it is that loves me."* If you love him then you will obey his great command to go into all the world and preach the gospel to all the nations.

What are we waiting for? Even these things I am writing can

make men and women in the church frustrated. Why? Simply put, it may tempt them to jump into a premature performance-driven Christianity, like many have become accustomed to, by trying to please God apart from faith. Anyone who claims they can produce a better life without belief in Christ's victory on the cross is premature and immature. Only faith in the Son of God will perfect a man or woman and cause them to do the works of God.

Anything outside of abiding in the vine of Christ will flat line and collapse. It takes people away from the fact that there is perfect ease in the Glory, as spoken by Ruth Ward Heflin. Based upon 13 years of experience in ministry, I can tell you when the Glory of God shows up and arises upon us in meetings as we do in the nations, no ministerial effort will be able to conjure up a drop of this unlimited power I am talking about. Without being head over heels in love with the person of Jesus, performance-based Christianity, at its best, produces nothing more than vain and futile exercises.

I hope the body of Christ will never be frustrated because they are not reaching their destination but rather enjoying the journey. I write this from my personal testimony. I can recall many days feeling restless because I didn't feel like I was fulfilling God's BIG will for my life. I only saw the big picture but never enjoyed the little steps getting there. And to be honest, where is there? What if the 'there' was here and now? What if something as simple as just showing acts of kindness to our neighbors could help us get outside ourselves, and bring the kingdom of God into people's lives?

When seeking to fulfill the call of God on your life, try not to be discouraged about seeing its full fruition like being in the big lights, in front of cameras, publishing books, and speaking on public platforms. Please know you fulfill God's joy every day you diligently seek to accomplish His will, and you find it in His word. The present is a gift from God and living in the future can't satisfy you like living today to its fullest.

What will it take for us to shake the world and every sphere of influence in every church, city, and nation? It will take nothing less than Isaiah 55. *Behold, thou shalt call a nation that thou knowest not, and nations that knew not thee shall run unto thee because of the Lord thy God, and for the Holy One of Israel; for he hath glorified thee* (Isaiah 55:5). Messiah will call into his kingdom a nation of the hungry and thirsty and they will quickly and gladly obey the call. The attraction will be the "glory" which God the Father has bestowed upon his Son and the love he has revealed through his people.

God's grace, glory, and nature have been infused in us at no cost, nothing, nada! FREE!

SOWING INTO ETERNITY

I found that the more I lose my desire for the temporal, and sow into eternity, I become more filled with eternal bliss! It's like I'm in the creamy, chocolaty center of the goodness of God, and my puckered lips are ready to kiss Abba Father's beautifully big face.

When you don't like the atmosphere over your city, go out and sow into the lives of the poor and watch an open Heaven form over your life! *But when thou makest a feast, call the poor, the maimed, the lame, the blind* (Luke 14:13). *The Spirit of the Lord [is] upon me, because he hath anointed me to preach the gospel to the poor* (Luke 4:18).

Bring ye all the tithes into the storehouse, that there may be meat in mine house, and prove me now herewith, saith the Lord of hosts, if I will not open you the windows of heaven, and pour you out a blessing, that there shall not be room enough to receive (Malachi 3:10). When you get to heaven, all your kind deeds will be rewarded with extra bricks of gold in your mansions. Your eternal rewards will shoot through the roof as you lose your time and resources in Jesus.

You may see great financial prosperity happen if you lose yourself in giving like a maniac. Then, watch the heavens open up over your life and wipe out all your debt. My wife and I have seen it happen, time after time. God is so faithful to His word and He will complete it. Even more intoxicating is the thought of the eternal rewards awaiting us.

I once walked into a door of heaven and saw mansions that Jesus made for his followers on the earth. This was after I had encountered a door going into hell to which I had been sentenced. I had a divine encounter in a dream that God used to save me from my backslidden state while in college. I knew heaven was so more worthwhile than the alternative. Heaven is pure eternal bliss, while hell is eternal pain and untold sorrow.

Hell looks like a terrifying place full of darkness and fire, and I knew once I went there, I would never get out! Other people that awaited being thrown into hell, were all on this downward spiral staircase, and none of them knew where they were going!

I cried out to God, "Please give me another chance!" Suddenly the force that was holding me captive against my will broke off of me. I ran out the door, and the Holy Spirit led me to kneel on a big rock and give my life to Jesus Christ.

After that moment, he directed me back to the judgment line, full of people that had died, which I reluctantly did. When I went back to the judgment line, people were there looking up everyone's information on computer systems. I figured it was some sort of technology in heaven that looked for these people and the work they've done.

When I was in that line, they told me, "Sorry, sir, you did not make it." I was forced to go through the doorway leading to hell.

This time they said to me, "Oh, I see, we had you mixed up with an old man name Ebenezer!" God was telling me to put off the old man and put on the new man, created in Christ. He was giving me another chance as Ebenezer received in the Christmas story.

That was the moment in my life when I would cash in all my chips on Jesus, willing to lose everything for him and knowing that I would find so much more than that dungeon where this backslidden prisoner had been held captive. I was invited to lose my life and find it eternally in Christ Jesus.

5

AS YOU GO, PREACH

JESUS DEBUTED HIS MINISTRY WITH THIS DECLARATION AND THEN he authorized and sent his followers to carry the same message everywhere they went. The message was clear — As you go, preach.

> And as you go, preach, saying, 'The kingdom of heaven is at hand' (Matthew 10:7).

> And he said unto them, Go ye into all the world, and preach the gospel to every creature (Mark 16:15).

If we approach this calling to preach the gospel with our minds focused upon delivering the message when we get to wherever we are going, then we will miss all the opportunities that await us along the way. It would be a mistake if we became so focused on what God will do later that we missed out on what God is doing now.

So, as you go, preach; don't wait until you get there.

Whereas ye know not what shall be on the morrow. For what is your life? It is even a vapour, that appeareth for a little time, and then vanisheth away (James 4:14). You don't know what your life will be like tomorrow. Life is like a fog quickly dissipated by the rising sun. Why put off to tomorrow what you can do today? Talk about losing your life! At the end of 2019, I made a wild commitment to Jesus, a pledge to spread the gospel to lost souls every single day!

Because Jesus gave me eternal life through faith and by his blood shed on the cross, I am compassionately compelled to serve him. I began to think about my life compared to eternity. As you are reading this book, we crossed over 350 days of nonstop evangelism and I have no intention of stopping with this track record. I don't need or seek your applause. I'm simply trying to tell you it is possible to live a life like this. I'm setting a standard that others can be inspired by and aspire to live the life of an evangelist. Paul's word for Timothy is a challenge for all of us. *But you be watchful in all things, endure afflictions, do the work of an evangelist, fulfill your ministry* (2 Timothy 4:5, emphasis added). You might not be Billy Graham or Ravi Zacharias, but ALL are called to do the work of an evangelist.

Your style of evangelism doesn't have to be on dramatic display with fireworks. A lot of times it is meeting people where they naturally gather, like when you are filling up the gas tank or shopping at the grocery store. Take advantage of all those natural places where people gather. When you are motivated by love for people, the eternal rewards will pay dividends you never imagined.

We live at the intersection between time and eternity. If

heaven did have time zones, then you could think about your first 100 million years in that heavenly place. You would be in total bliss and after that 100 million years it would only calculate to a short period of time. What? 100 million years is a short time? Well, yes absolutely compared to eternity. Next, ponder the next 200 million years there in eternity. Once you reach that point, you're still alive, having the time of your life with Jesus Christ and with all your saved loved ones, not to mention all the cool people you'll meet there. How about after that? The next 500 million years? Do you get my point? So, if life is like a vapor here on earth compared to eternity, certainly I should work as hard as I can while I am here on earth to build eternal rewards awarded by Jesus.

WHERE WILL YOU SPEND ETERNITY?

How about the flip side of this equation? Picture all those years I mentioned above and think about people that will spend the rest of eternity in the fire of hell, a fire that cannot be quenched, and where the worm does not die (Mark 9:48). When Jesus described hell, he mentioned that there will be weeping and gnashing of teeth. Demons will literally torture people for eons (Matthew 13:42). Those that go there with unrepentant sin or full rejection of Jesus Christ, they can never get out! Since God created us eternal beings, we can't die. Sadly, these people will experience eternal death for the rest of eternity, in absolute agony, no ability to breathe, no ability to quench their thirst, no ability to eat again, and no ability to rest or sleep.

If I saw a man running towards me who was about to plummet off the edge of a precipice, I would run and tackle him.

I would do anything I could to stop him from leaping and dying. It should be the same in our love for the lost people around us. I once heard a preacher describe eternity in hell like this. Imagine every thousand years someone takes a handkerchief and wipes it across Mount Everest. He gently swipes it across the top of the mountain every thousand years. Once, that mountain was completely eroded by the slight brush of the handkerchief during those years that will be the duration and fate of a person in hell and it will only be their first day! These verses paint the picture with a brutally dark color.

> They will be punished with everlasting destruction and shut out from the presence of the Lord and from the glory of his might (II Thessalonians 1:9).

Sodom and Gomorrah and the surrounding towns gave themselves up to sexual immorality and perversion. (Jude 1:7). They serve as an example of those who suffer the punishment of eternal fire.

Jesus describes the fate of a damned soul that thought they were saved but Jesus tells them to depart from him for he never knew them, even though they had performed wonderful works in his name (Mathew 7:21-23). In verse 24 he cautioned those listening to him to avoid that horrifying scenario. By hearing his words and putting them into practice, they avoid the fires of hell. That person is a wise man who built his life upon the rock. Obedience is proof we love Jesus and have not hidden any form of lawlessness in our life!

Spending eternity in the worst place imaginable, how ghastly would that be? It's horrifying to think about it! What is mind-boggling is that God made it easy to take that eternal escape route, leading directly to heaven. Unfortunately, too many refuse the gift because they are not willing to humble themselves like children and receive eternal life as a free gift (Matthew 18:4). Just repent from sin and put your faith in Jesus Christ. It's that easy! It's the greatest retirement plan you've ever heard of and it lasts forever. However, we will not be retiring because we will be reigning with Jesus Christ and we will have an infinite amount of assignments to accomplish and fun to be experienced.

PEOPLE IN YOUR NEIGHBORHOOD

At the end of November 2019, I got on the YouTube search engine and looked for people who had been to heaven and hell, especially those who had been on Sid Roth's show. It made me think. I did not want to lose my life for Christ. I wanted to tell everyone I met about Jesus. I was being motivated by the reality of eternity. Having my eyes glued to eternity, the value of a lost soul became preeminent in my thinking. I could not shake it.

It all began on Black Friday 2019. I had years of street evangelism experience under my belt, including international mission trips to 30 countries around the world. My wife and I went to Israel 20 times on assignment from Jesus and we have been in full-time vocational ministry since 2007. As I was praying about our next international journey, the Lord reminded me of a dream he gave me that created heartache for my nation, America.

The first time I experienced this dream it was loud in my head, as I was coming out of sleep. The sound I heard was a song and the lyrics imposed a question. "Who are the people in your neighborhood?" That song was on air in the 1980s when I was a young boy. It's probably one of the catchiest songs ever made! Not only did it touch a special part of my childhood, but I had completely forgotten the song! I had to Google it just to find out where this song came from. In his infinite wisdom, Holy Spirit sang a secular song to me, with a message contained in the lyrics, just for me, and now it's for you.

> "Well, they're the people that you meet
> When you're walking down the street
> They're the people that you meet each day!"[1]

If I could put 100 cry emojis into this book, I would put them right here. At that moment I cried, thinking of its meaning, once again.

The Lord God Jehovah Almighty was telling me that he wanted me to talk to people every day as I go because he cares so much for people. They are the people you meet when you're walking down the street and they are in your neighborhood.

Jesus had chosen the twelve who became his disciples. Jesus was a preacher and now the twelve became preachers. While preparing them to go, Jesus said, "And as you go, preach, saying, "The kingdom of heaven is at hand. Heal the sick, cleanse the lepers, raise the dead, cast out demons. Freely you have received, freely give." (Matthew 10:7, 8)

I found it interesting when he said, "As you go, preach..." Jesus means business, the business of saving the world. As the disciples went out to preach, so should we. Everywhere you go, you are being sent by him. So, why are you keeping your mouth

shut? We give our accolades to miracle ministers who are doing all the work for us when many of them want you to do it. Jesus wants power evangelism to be manifested in our lives, everywhere we walk.

Why? Because he loves people! In John 3:16 it doesn't say God loved the world; it says that he SO loved the world! If we love God, we will carry His broken heart for the lost sheep. We will be excited like the prodigal son's father when the lost children come home.

It was Black Friday when a UPS truck drives into my neighborhood. I rushed outside to meet the driver and I prophesied over him! He happened to be a believer and he received the word. The word was accurate, and it blessed him so much and I followed up by praying for him. Once again, I became addicted to evangelism!

The next day, I went out and prayed for another worker in my neighborhood. That boy ended up receiving Jesus Christ as his personal Lord and Savior, right there. I believe it was the next day that my good friend, Alex Parkinson came to visit us with his dear wife, Jordan. He accompanied me when I went to my local grocery store and conducted, what I like to call servant evangelism.

Now, we are taking evangelism to the next level and that is in making disciples. I encourage every reader reading this book to research the cutting edge DMM discipleship making movement in Christianity today. We are modeling the following: Finding the man or woman of influence in a community, leading them to Jesus, discipling them, and raising them up as the home church leader in their neighborhood utilizing their own house as the place of meeting.

Then, they continue weekly discovery Bible studies and in turn win all of their neighbors to Jesus right where they live! A good place to start learning about this groundbreaking evangelism movement is by subscribing to *Missions Frontiers* magazine. If you are not already, you must. It's not about how many people we can get to say the sinner's prayer, but how many people we lead to Jesus that will now raise up a Bible study to win their friends and family to Jesus right where they live!

ADVENTURES IN EVANGELISM AT THE GROCERY STORE

I love our ministry partners, so much. During that week, some love offerings came in and we decided to go to the self-checkout line at the grocery store. Once we arrived, we randomly paid for people's groceries. As the person checked out, I would walk up and pay for their groceries.

Luke 16:9 says, "Use your worldly resources to benefit others and make friends. Then, when your possessions are gone, they will welcome you to an eternal home." Some of the commentaries interpret it to mean that resources are given to us so we can help people find repentance and faith in Jesus Christ. This is Jesus' insinuation.[2]

I wonder if the meaning of this parable is that we use our worldly wealth to preach the gospel to people and since Jesus is the only one that saves us we will get to chill out in heaven, enjoying the heavenly mansions with those we won to Jesus!

So, when we put money in the machine to pay for their groceries the reactions were always priceless. People often wonder why we're doing it. It's clear. It opens up the door for me to gleefully share my testimony and invite them to come to know Jesus Christ as their Savior.

On a side note, we try to help people understand why they need Jesus. We live in a culture where morality is abandoned, so using the 10 commandments and asking them if they've ever committed those sins is a good way to bring conviction. Paul said that the law made him conscious of sin. *What shall we say then? Is the law sin? Certainly not! On the contrary, I would not have known sin except through the law. For I would not have known covetousness unless the law had said, "You shall not covet"* (Romans 7:7).

The love of God is a powerful motivation for change, but people need to know why they need him and know that without him they are going to hell, to live there forever. Even though he loves the sinner, if they reject him, he will reject them for they have chosen the way of sin and death. People need to know why they need him and where they are going if they don't have him. They need Christ as their savior and Lord. In the classic words of John 3:16, "For God so loved the world that he gave his only begotten son so that whosoever believes in him will not perish but have everlasting life." Those who believe will receive and will not perish. Those who do not believe will perish. In a lot of the prophetic streams, this form of evangelism is not welcomed, but God is bringing it back to the center. Repentance is a beautiful thing and it should not have the negative stigma it has in other places. Repentance is turning your back 180° on sin and refusing to go back. It's not just changing your mind like so many of the Christian apologists emphasize. Sam Storms says that repentance is more than a change of mind, as some would say. It is a change of direction, a change of life, and action.[3] It's being heartbroken over sin like God is heartbroken over it.

In the grocery store, we would huddle in prayer with people after buying their groceries and the Holy Ghost would fall upon us. That shows me that God likes it when we go and bless our local community. At one point, I was on the ground under the power of God. Also, we were distributing free Bibles and Christian literature, and no one was kicking us out of the store for solicitation! Favor comes with a price, sometimes.

We've had people cry tears and we've had people elated with joy when we do this type of ministry. At the end of the night, Alex and I were about to depart when we both had the same idea. Alex asked me if we should push the envelope by seeing if we could preach the gospel over the intercom to all those in the store. Insert a big LOL right, there, right? My response was, "What are the chances?"

I felt our chances were fairly good. I asked someone in authority if I could say something over the intercom before we left, something about the good news. She was a Christian lady from Thailand who put her daughter in a private Christian school and to my surprise, we got a 'yes.' She walked over to the intercom, picked up the phone, and handed it to me. I was dumbfounded. That evening, she allowed me to preach the glorious gospel of Jesus Christ to an entire grocery store, while I was intoxicated in the Glory of God. Other times, I've gone back to do it again, since there was an open door of favor. On some of my flights, I've even preached to all the people on a plane. I asked the stewardess if she would announce that anyone who wanted free coffee could see me on the layover and I would treat them. I've had the opportunity to share Jesus with people, applying this outrageous evangelism idea in airports. I've never been turned down by a stewardess because people want to get in on being a blessing.

ADVENTURES IN EVANGELISM AT THE COFFEE SHOP

We love to do this at Starbucks. I know what you are thinking, boycott them because they do a lot of bad things. However, what if we treat everybody to coffee and it gives us a preaching platform? Well, it did! We took some of our money and put hundreds of dollars in a gift card and played a little game with the barista. I told him that we were doing random acts of kindness, only for the indoor customers. I told him to use the gift card to take care of everyone's coffee and tell them where we are, in case they want to thank us. 10 out of 10 times they say yes! People want to get involved in being a blessing.

We have had incredible experiences at Starbucks! Normally, I park at the table where they announce drinks are ready. I share my testimony and the good news with every customer whose eyes are wide open with joy, all because we treated them. God gave me a word of knowledge for one girl going through the line. I told her about drawing pictures of horses when she was little. She said it was an accurate word. I asked her if she believed in Jesus. She responded by saying she was agnostic. It's amazing what one gift of love and one word of knowledge will do for an agnostic or an atheist. It's a genuine expression of God's love that they will remember the rest of their life while demonstrating how real God is.

On another occasion, we had the opportunity to pray for two Egyptian girls who we bought coffee for. As we were praying, one of the sisters started hysterically laughing and could not hold it back. My friend with me discerned that the Holy Spirit was filling her, and she was going through deliverance. The Holy Ghost showed up, with power, and the other sister could not believe she was cracking up during prayer.

Another Egyptian woman saw what we were doing and begged me to sit with them. Are you ready for something supernatural? She said that I had such an overwhelming peace coming out of my eyes and it felt like the peace was touching her, all over her body, and she asked me how I got that peace. Oh, how wonderful the Holy Spirit is! When we arise and shine for our light has come and the glory of the Lord has risen upon us, nations come to the brightness of our rising! (Isaiah 60:1)

There have been people who came through the coffee line that we treated, and God would supernaturally heal their body. We've even prayed for people who didn't know God and the Holy Spirit would fill them and they became intoxicated in his presence. Those people asked if we drugged them! In the old saying, there truly is no high like the Most High.

I remember the time when I met a kid in a coffee shop. He was shocked at the accuracy of the word of knowledge we shared with him. I saw a pictorial vision of him mailing postcards to distant relatives, trying to drop the mail in a red mailbox. Whenever he tried to mail a postcard to his dad, he could never do it. He shockingly said, "I'm from Germany." He said that the mailboxes in Germany are red. He said that he does mail postcards to his relatives, but he wanted to send one to his dad but couldn't because he was bitter at him. That night he got filled with the Holy Spirit as we proclaimed the gospel of Jesus Christ to Him, with power.

AS YOU GO, PREACH • 63

Isn't God's love amazing when we lose our life for him? It has become common for me to walk into theaters, barbershops, restaurants, and stand up and preach the gospel to every single person and at the conclusion invite them to accept a personal relationship with Jesus Christ. While big churches and ministries come together and wait for stadium events to happen, which are mostly Spirit-filled believers, we're already preaching to the lost people, numbers of people that could easily fill those stadiums every day. I'm not saying I'm better. I'm just saying don't wait for the next stadium event. Jesus is moving on the streets and you are the invited speaker!!!

Often, people ask me how to do I get so much boldness? I tell them I do it with my leg shaking but God still shows up. I always have to push through that barrier called the fear of man. However, the more I practice, the easier it becomes. What matters is not the fear in front of me, but the fruit that comes from lives being saved, saved for eternity. Fear is a fake spider! It is not real. It is an illusion not worth considering.

ADVENTURES IN EVANGELISM AT THE LOCAL HIGH SCHOOL

The residents in my community complain about how bad our high school is. It is bad, I will not lie. There are gangs and rough people there but all they need is some real love in the world. Instead of complaining about problems in our community, why don't we become the solution? I'm about to see Jesus turn the high school upside down. You just watch and see what happens.

After I started going to the streets every day, God gave me an idea to preach by using a loudspeaker. I wanted to reach all the 1700 high school students, as they waited outside for the buses. I stand on a public sidewalk in front of the school to make it legal. I've held signs up saying, "Jesus is coming." "Jesus died for you and will you live for him?" I've told them that their lives are valuable to God, encouraging them not to listen to the people telling them to kill themselves.

God gave me an idea to go to the local fast-food restaurants when school let out and because of the generosity of our partners and friends were able to buy the students food. I've had numerous opportunities to pray for local high school students. God is changing lives. Our partners helped us to buy $600 worth of Chick-fil-A for reaching the kids and guess what? The local basketball team showed up and devoured the lunch we bought them. They invited me to the game that night and I came with my 'Jesus is coming' sign. Because of my radical enthusiasm for Jesus, I got invited to a local Bible study, led by young people from the school. I preached and gave my testimony and God did the miracles. Over 20 people received Jesus as their Savior! After all of that, I have favor with some of the immensely popular people at that school.

All over the city, I meet young people that asked me if I'm the "Jesus" guy that stands on the street corner with the loudspeaker or the sign. I saw one high school student that I ministered to become bold and he's beginning to share videos on his Instagram account about how Jesus is coming soon. The Lord is showing me that I am making a difference in these kids' lives because they need someone to look up to. Many are getting saved.

God has even been blowing up my story on one social media platform. One of my videos hit over 1.2 million views and, often, people ask me how they can be saved. We just need to figure out how to reach people on our streets and through digital evange-lism. God will use everything He can and by any way He can bring the lost to Christ.

I'll never forget the time we led a young kid to the Lord who was on the streets. That summer we discipled him, teaching him the ways of Jesus. Right after he surrendered his life to Christ, he had an incredible vision. This illustrates how much Jesus loves new believers. While he and some friends were sitting around the campfire, he saw Jesus Christ in an open vision. He said he saw white robes and everything the book of Revelation described concerning Jesus, but he could not determine what his eyes looked like. One of the other kids we were discipling came over and hit him on the back, shouting, "Brother his eyes are fire." He said that and immediately fire came out of Jesus' eyes and enveloped him. The only thing he could do was run around the field like a wild man! Jesus! That's my boss!

EVANGELISM ON THE STREETS

I remember a time when we went out and something cool happened! I was preaching from my megaphone on a public sidewalk at the intersection, during the Covid-19 crisis. We were having church on the streets. As people waited at the traffic light, with their car windows down, they would hear my testimony and the glorious gospel of Jesus Christ.

At one point, a young man came up to flirt with the girls on our team. He didn't know what he was getting into. The Holy Ghost showed up as we began to pray that God would heal his back pain. He said he prayed to Allah, but my friend insisted telling him that we pray to Jesus! My friend felt where his back was sticking out and, as he prayed, his back went inward again. His back was completely healed in the very presence of God.

The power of the Holy Ghost touched our team and it was so powerful that we were all lying down on the sidewalk, in absolute euphoria. The presence of God was so strong that I had to preach from the megaphone while laying down. One lady was waiting at the traffic light and she began to scream praise to Jesus, over and over and over. She was undone by what we were doing. Even the mayor of our city passed by numerous times. He supports what we were doing because he is a born-again Christian. I felt the power of the Holy Ghost stronger on the street than in many services I do. It shows you he is ready to bring revival.

Smith Wigglesworth would say if the spirit is not moving, then I'll move the spirit. We had a similar experience on a mission trip to Cardiff Wales. The whole team got blasted in the Holy Ghost and everyone was knocked out on the ground. Bystanders were coming up and asking us if we were on drugs or protesting. One girl had the bright idea to invite the bystanders to lay down with us and they began to get filled with the Holy Ghost and laugh hysterically.

I'm telling you there is a revival on the streets right now! You only need to go and press forward until you see it happen! Will you get made fun of? Probably, and quite frequently! Will people say all kinds of false things about you? Absolutely! Jesus said they would. It happens to us more than you could imagine. But Jesus said, "Blessed are you when they revile and persecute you and say all kinds of evil against you falsely for My sake. Rejoice and be exceedingly glad, for great *is* your reward in heaven, for so they persecuted the prophets who were before you." (Mathew

5:11, 12) I can assure you that the glorious rewards you will forever experience will outweigh the negative things people say about you.

SADDENED BY THE FRIVOLOUS

It saddens me that Christians waste valuable hours debating on Facebook with other believers, while their local high school students are going to hell. Do you know what that is called? That's called 'sin' and I'm not afraid to say it. When is the church going to wake up and realize that Jesus is serious, and that time is running out before he comes back?

Steve Hill, the evangelist at the Brownsville revival, once said that many Christians were so mad because some states wanted to remove the Ten Commandments from their courthouses, when they've already removed the ten commandments from their hearts.

Those same people break the second commandment, making idolatry while busying themselves with insignificant things on social media, when they have abandoned their prayer life and act like hell does not exist.

They are like the Pharisees who strain at a gnat, but we swallow a camel. There are people on Facebook who get so ferocious with someone whose theology isn't correct, belittling them and demanding them to change their theology, and at the same time, they don't love a drug addict in their neighborhood. They don't let them know that Jesus loves them and can save them. It is appalling to see how Satan blinds so many Christians, convincing them to be so busy with unfruitful religious activity, including posting photos of their latest recipes on Instagram, and the photo they posted of a lost soul that got saved on a mission trip was a decade ago.

Some of the people that argue on social media are probably uncles and aunts that did not have a job since the first George Bush was President. They complain about being tired for weeks because they had to watch their nieces and nephews for a day. I feel they could use some vitamin B and read their gospel again because the great commission is not the great suggestion. People get ridiculously high minded and all-mighty behind their keyboards but, in person, there's not one iota of backbone in their body.

It's easier to be a disgruntled Christian, concerned about how the world is getting so dark than it is to be a proactive Christian going into your community and letting your light shine in the darkness and teach people the ways of God. Many get so excited because they believe a one billion youth harvest is coming but they don't lift a finger to help one dying soul.

There is a disease in the world called sin and we have the cure. Jesus is the cure for what ails the world! I know it sounds like I'm being tough but correcting the modern-day church is needed. If all of us would stand before Jesus in eternity, we would see how many opportunities we lost in sharing the gospel with people. God is about to change that!

Would you put down your book and say this prayer. "Dear Lord, please forgive me for being hypocritical. Help me to read your word constantly and let it change me from the inside out. Let me truly learn how to love and lay my life down for the cross of Jesus. Amen!"

6

THE ECSTASY OF LOVING YOUR HATERS

You have heard that it was said, 'You shall love your neighbor and hate your enemy. But I say to you, love your enemies, bless those who curse you, do good to those who hate you, and pray for those who spitefully use you and persecute you (Mathew 5:43, 44).

AFTER A MORNING RAIN OR A DEWY NIGHT, THE FLOWERS AND THE blades of grass are bejeweled with silvery water droplets. The tiniest water balls form nearly perfect spheres, each a tiny lens that brings a view of the background scenes within its curved showcase. There is a peculiar grace to the dewdrop. The sun shares its cheerfulness with the crystal heart of the drop.

Love descends like dew on the red rose and the sharp blades of grass, causing life to spring forth in all its beauty. Love, like the miracle of the dewdrop, is a transforming power, changing prickly flowers into exquisite wonder, made possible by the power of love.

In her autobiography, St. Thérèse, the Little Flower,

describes her search for a mission in life. While she was engaged in prayerful contemplation of the Scriptures in the solitude of the Carmelite monastery, she discovered her call was to live out the words described by the Apostle Paul in 1 Corinthians 15 on the preeminence of love. "In near ecstasy, Thérèse realized her mission in life was to love all of humanity, beginning with some difficult members in her community, and, as she expressed it, she intended to cast flowers upon each individual in the world. Eventually, she called her spirituality 'The Little Way.' "[1]

A DIFFERENT KIND OF LOVE

In the opening scripture, Jesus is not dealing with the Law but with the scribes' interpretation of the Law. The fierce fanaticism of the Pharisaic Jews, like a clanging cymbal, rang with dictates of hatred against the Gentiles. 'It has been said,' with those words captured in the Sermon on the Mount, Jesus' transforming touch brought fresh life to the Law, creating a prophetic understanding of the energy of inward spirituality manifested in dynamic love. As one voice, Jesus and Paul proclaim this supreme, all-including commandment, which is the power of love. The world is a better place when we love the haters.

The title of this book, *Ecstatic Christianity,* is so awe-inspiring I decided to dedicate this chapter to what it means to love the haters. We serve a Savior who asked his Father to forgive those who crucified Him on the cross. His life should inspire us to love the unlovable, unlike the world's concept of love.

Jesus said, "My peace I give you, not as the world gives, do, I give to you" (John 14:27). The peace that comes from proactively following Christ's teachings 'to love our enemies' is so opposed to the world that it doesn't make sense. Throughout history, we can find multiple stories illustrating when love shines bright, lives are blessed and changed. The world does not understand that kind of love, a love that causes people to become friends with the murderer of a family member, to the extent of forgiving them, thus saving their life. It's a love and peace from another world. It comes from the Father's heart.

We live in a world where the rule is, 'watch out for your own interests.' We sue people who have offended us, hurt us, or damaged us in some way. We malign those who have lower standards than ours or who are not like us. Too many people live by harmful competitive natures, not realizing how their actions cause emotional hurt. It's easy to be a jerk towards those who have done us wrong, but it's difficult to bless them with gracious acts like giving them a gift card or other demonstrations of love. God is the supreme example of real love, not worldly love.

"In this the love of God was manifested toward us, that God has sent His only begotten Son into the world, that we might live through Him. In this is love, not that we loved God, but that He loved us and sent His Son to be the propitiation for our sins" (I John 4:9. 10).

HEAPING COALS OF FIRE

The church often forgets that golden nugget, buried in their Bible, a treasure unveiled by Jesus and preached by Paul the Apostle. "If your enemy is hungry, feed him;

If he is thirsty, give him a drink; For in so doing you will heap coals of fire on his head" (Romans 12:20). The traditional hatred of your enemy is repudiated by the words of Jesus and Paul. A spark of love will melt the hardened heart, liquifying them into repentance.

Do you remember that the book's reoccurring theme is about the ecstasy of losing your life and the euphoria of finding it? The elements of love and pride do not mix. Until you lay down your pride, you cannot influence others. If you love those who love you, why should you get credit for that? (Luke 6:32). God's love, which should be our love, does not conform to the love displayed in the world. Lay down your pride and let God's love flow through you to others. If you do this, in His name, you will become an agent of change and God will reward you.

Putting coals on your enemy's head is not literal. It does not mean you burn their head with burning coals or that self-avenging is acceptable; it means that you show them the way. Coals of fire bring light into the darkness and help them see the pathway before them. The Expositor's Greek New Testament offers further insight into this verse. "The burning pain is the shame and remorse which the man feels whose hostility is repaid by love. This is the only kind of vengeance the Christian is at liberty to contemplate."[2]

In my early years of serving the Lord, I recall when the enemy tried to sow discord and division in a friendship I had, a friendship that was dear to my heart. Without going into the details, my heart was hurt, and I wanted to break the spirit of division that existed between us.

I was resolved to do something so radical for my friend, which didn't make sense to most people. My wife and I decided to give him our only vehicle. That's right, you read it correctly. We gave him our car. The gesture was done in loving-kindness and received with deep appreciation. The heaping coals of love healed and restored our friendship. Since then, the Lord has been kind to us. Twice we have been given new vehicles. In an extreme way, the Lord rewarded us for this radical example of Christ's love.

GIVE AND IT SHALL BE GIVEN TO YOU

On another occasion, my wife and I were preaching in Huntsville, Alabama. The car we were driving was a clunker, and there were times when it would not start. Even after the first seven times of turning the key in the ignition, it would not start. A friend of mine came to say goodbye and noticed that I was having trouble starting my car. At that time, he was the general manager of a car dealership. The Lord spoke to him, telling him to give us the Honda Odyssey on his property. Besides that, the Lord put it on his heart to fix it up and he put in a new engine. It was luxurious and, on top of everything else, he installed a DVD player in the car, for our children.

The amazing thing was that the Holy Spirit had spoken to the pastor's wife to help get us a Honda Odyssey. She had no idea that the Holy Spirit was simultaneously talking to that general manager about the Honda Odyssey.

When the general manager told the pastor what God put on his heart to do for us, the pastor's wife wept. The church committed to taking up a love offering to help get the vehicle fixed up for us. It was a genuinely nice used vehicle, and they drove it up to our home, with a bow on it. My family was stupefied, overwhelmed by their love. As the Bible says, the Lord will reward you when you show kindness to an enemy, and that is what he did for us.

GO THE EXTRA MILE

Recently when I was doing street evangelism, a young man got mad at me. He threatened me, telling me he was going to pop me if I didn't leave them alone. I immediately told him and his friends that I would love to treat them for lunch at MacDonald's. It didn't work out at that time because they were in a hurry. Not long afterward, I saw them at Dollar General and bought bottles of cold Gatorade for all of them.

Countless times we have seen God's incredible provision increase when we love the unlovable. It's so easy to forget Jesus' incredible demands. Remember when he said if someone forces you to go one mile, go two miles. If you are sued in court and your shirt is taken from you, give your coat, too (Mathew 5:40, 41). The Jesus Principle is explicit. Give to him who asks you, and from him who wants to borrow from you do not turn away (Mathew 5:42). A loving heart gives to haters and the needy, to the unworthy and the worthy ones.

God often directs me to pray for my persecutors and enemies. So, I've come up with a clever prayer that protects me from bitterness. "Lord, please be kind to that person and save them, and when we both get to Heaven, put our mansions right next to each other!" I am smiling as I am writing.

I can assure you when we get to heaven, we will see how upside down it is compared to our self-centered world. I am certain when we arrive, there will be no more divisions, denominations, sects, or anything that divides God's people. We will

love each other and want to serve one another. In conclusion, reflect on the potency of Paul's words to the Colossians.

"Therefore, as the elect of God, holy and beloved, put on tender mercies, kindness, humility, meekness, long-suffering; bearing with one another, and forgiving one another, if anyone has a complaint against another; even as Christ forgave you, so you also must do. But above all these things put on love, which is the bond of perfection" (Colossians 3:12-14).

7

LOSING YOURSELF IN JESUS

The secret of spiritual success is a hunger that persists...It is an awful condition to be satisfied with one's spiritual attainments...God was and is looking for hungry, thirsty people." (Smith Wigglesworth)

THE DESERT IS THE PLACE OF DEATH AND LIFE. STONE FIELDS merge into sandy plains and boiling soil. Sandstorms descend upon desert plains, covering the beloved oasis with a blanket of sand. No shadow for miles. No place to hide from the burning sun.

Suddenly, the wind stirs, and hurricane-force winds rearrange the desert dunes into brilliant formations of exquisite beauty. Could such a place have been beautiful at all? Although the soil looks dry, there is still some vegetation. The land changes before you know it. One place has grass and grazing camels, and several miles away is nothing except the sun and blistering sand.

All creation worships the Creator in their unique way, from mountain tops to frozen tundra, from blue oceans to desert sands. The whistling dunes are the desert phenomena as wind pass over the dunes, causing a singing sound. Sometimes, it sounds like a deep groaning hum produced by tiny grains of sand rolling down the dune.

The immense desert, empty as a pocket, but inspired with promises. The desert humbles the soul, leaving it to cry out in thirst and hunger. Streams in the desert, as life flows through the arid places. This is the beginning, your beginning of a life unattached from lifeless religion and selfish living.

Night encompasses the desert. It came suddenly with flashes of shooting stars decorating the sky. In the clear air, the desert moon reminds us that in those desert places, battles were fought, enemies were conquered, and God was speaking. *And the Lord spoke to Moses in the desert* (Numbers 1:1, Douay-Rheims Bible).

When men look up at the desert sky and see nothing but endless infinity, they have always had a driving and desperate urge to see God, experience God. On a desert floor, Jacob lay prostrate on the ground with his head on a rock, awakening to a ladder extended upwards into the heavens while surrounded by angels. You never know what might happen in the desert. God is there, and he is not silent.

As the sun rises in the desert, one cannot tell where heaven ends, and the earth begins. What draws us to the desert? Pebbles of sand mixed with crystallized tears. It is our search for reality and intimacy and a longing to be relevant in an irrelevant world. Come, Holy Spirit. The winds are blowing like a mighty wind.

The Indonesian revival of 1965 is peppered with supernatural stories. This story is the beginning of stories. "Four nights before the nearly successful communist coup in Indonesia in 1965, God sovereignly began pouring out His Spirit in a small town on the little-known island of Timor. He alerted the Christians to pray, and the country was remarkably spared. Immediately, evangelistic teams of laymen were formed and began traveling throughout Timor and surrounding islands proclaiming the gospel, healing the sick, and raising the dead. The miracles that followed the day of Pentecost, when the Spirit first came "like a mighty wind," have been reenacted in our day."

PARTNERING WITH GOD

We crave for the mighty wind to blow again across our desert land. At this time, there is a dire need for a revelation of intimacy with the Holy Spirit and how we can lose ourselves in the Son of God. The Son desires to draw His sons and daughters to the Father. There is a significant surge of revelation released from heaven for those who need it. Hunger will access it, embrace it. Having faith that Jesus has won it all for us is a critical key for our future.

God intends to flood the atmosphere with a heavenly downpour of reformation and revival, but it will not happen without corporate faith. Faith unleashes hopeful expectation that Kingdom power will be released in His people. God needs no invitation to do it. If only the body of Christ would collectively reach the place of an undeniable, unified commitment, to cultivating spiritual hunger on the earth. If we make that commitment, we will see something more significant than the first Great

Awakening. The spiritual awakening would even shake the Muslim world before the return of Christ.

Slithering across the floor, the enemy seeks to stir up hatred toward the Muslims, both in our country and the rest of the Muslim world. The Lord will resist this demonic effort causing them to collapse in utter failure. The Lord is releasing a special love in the body of Christ for Muslims. It will require you to lay down all prejudice and accept God's love to experience and exhibit this kind of love.

In the last decade, I prophesied that Ishmael was coming home, and there would be revival among the Muslims. As brothers, Isaac and Ishmael once stood together when they buried their father Abraham in Machpelah's cave. A day will come when prophetically, they will stand together again as one (Genesis 25:9). There is a revival in Iran, as Christianity has become the fastest-growing religion in Iran. With a passion for the Muslims' salvation, we watch missionaries spread throughout Islamic countries for the cause of Christ. It is time for Ishmael to come home! God wants his house full.[1]

CHANGING THE ATMOSPHERE

Individually and corporately, the bride is awakening to the fact that we are called to walk along earthly settings, carrying the atmosphere of the kingdom wherever we go. For the sons of God to settle for anything less would be unappealing and unacceptable. We were created for more than the ordinary. C. S. Lewis found the needle in the haystack when he wrote these words. "If we find ourselves with a desire that nothing in this world can satisfy, the most probable explanation is that we were made for another world."[2] When we learn to partner with God, we enter into an exhilarating lifestyle that will transform the culture and initiate a shift in the atmosphere. When that happens, heaven invades earth.

Concerning transforming atmospheres, I remember when we went out around midnight to minister to gothic kids in a local park. This particular night, I had a sense of boldness, expecting God was going to do something spectacular! Boldly, I walked up to a group of gothic teenagers talking with each other while smoking cigarettes. I introduced myself, saying, "Hey everyone, we are here tonight to give away free dream interpretations. Would you like for us to interpret any of yours?" It was a 'drop the mic' moment. They were so excited, and many teenagers came to my team and me to see if God could interpret their dreams. He did! He was reading their mail.

A friend and I were ready to take it to the next level. We asked if any of them had pain in their body. One young man had severe joint pain in his hands, knees, and elbows. For years he suffered from it, and it appeared there was no diagnosis for his condition. I looked at the kids and asked them if they had ever seen a miracle. I proceeded to ask if they would like to see one right now. In unison, they said, "Yes!" We prayed for the young man, and at first, nothing happened, but we did not stop there! We pressed in and laid hands on him again and prayed. I asked him to check the pain in his hands and knees. To his amazement, the pain that once racked his body was gone! The church turned off this young man, but he committed to return to a relationship with Jesus and the church!

A HEAVENLY INVASION

It is our mandate! Walk into enemy territory and subdue it, allowing the kingdom of God to be manifest with power. We are called to display the kingdom of God until the earth looks like the kingdom! What happened that night, should be a normal life for believers whose ears lean into the chest of Jesus, hearing His pulse beat for more disciples to be shaped into the image of God. This is everyday life for me, all to the glory of God.

We should constantly listen to the longing in God's heart, desiring that His eternal house be filled with God's family, bought by Jesus' shed blood! How exciting! There are too many Christians living in a "pie in the sky when you die" mentality of heaven when in reality, we aren't going up, heaven is coming down! The millennial reign of Christ will be on earth.

What is the remedy for this passive reality? The church cannot afford to sit back at this hour and let the world continue to say we are weak, lacking in love, and crippled by ignorance. We can't keep allowing droves of humanity to turn to the occult as a viable scientific alternative to narrow-minded religion. There is nothing scientific or supernatural about the occult, but it is just fallen demons' flawed attempt to mimic the anointing or the glory. For years we have tolerated the culture around us as they pursue other religions and the occult because they have not recognized God in the church. Once again, I ask what is the remedy?

The answer is an unending passion and compassion arising in the bride's heart, which "many waters cannot quench." The leaven of the kingdom will spread beyond the church's four walls, multiplying throughout the surrounding culture until the whole world becomes leavened. The socio-cultural effect of the kingdom of God will be comprehensive. Just as yeast works until the dough has completely risen, God's kingdom's ultimate benefit will be worldwide. "The earth will be filled with the knowledge of the glory of the LORD, as the waters cover the sea." (Habakkuk 2:14)

There will be a marketplace revival with the likes we have never seen. There will be a youth revival the world has never experienced because all the saint's prayers, for centuries, are about to pour out on this generation.

TWO PARABLES, ONE MESSAGE

"Another parable put he forth to them, saying, The kingdom of heaven is like to a grain of mustard seed, which a man took, and sowed in his field: Which indeed is the least of all seeds: but when it is grown, it is the greatest among herbs, and becomes a tree, so that the birds of the air come and lodge in the branches thereof" (Matthew 13:31, 32).

"Another parable spake He unto them; The Kingdom of Heaven is like unto leaven, which a woman took, and hid in three measures of meal, till the whole was leavened." (Matthew 13:33)

The parable of the mustard seed is designed to show that God's community is destined to advance from a small beginning into a vast multitude with extensive growth in every direction. The parable of the leaven, on the other hand, demonstrates how the specific influences of the kingdom gradually penetrate the whole culture, the entire mass is scrupulously changed into that spiritual condition which qualifies it for admittance into the kingdom. The Expositor's Greek New Testament creates a beautiful summary of the two parables. "Both these parables show how thoroughly Jesus was aware that great things grow from minute beginnings. How different his idea of the coming of the kingdom, from the current one of a glorious, mighty empire coming suddenly, full-grown! Instead, a mustard seed, a little leaven!"[3]

Though the world languishes in a dormant state, supernatural powers are released by the Holy Spirit upon his people, leading to the transformation of humanity from a dead, chunk of mass into a glorious body, penetrated by a quickening influence. *"But if the Spirit of him that raised Jesus from the dead dwell in you, he that raised Christ from the dead shall also quicken your mortal bodies by his Spirit that dwelleth in you"* (Romans 8:11). We can expect nations to be saved! God's glory will spread to parks, campuses, movie theaters, and many other places where people gather. The Warrior Bride will be the conduit God uses to bring that leaven of the kingdom spreading it through the media, the arts, and entertainment.

COME, HOLY SPIRIT

How can we be conduits for change? God gave me a dream, and in it he clearly showed me that the obstacles preventing us from the next level of revival in America are fear of man and inexperience with the Holy Spirit.

The Holy Spirit is my greatest love in life. My heart is

captivated by Him and His beautiful presence, and I become more ecstatic as our relationship matures and becomes stronger and stronger. When you get closer to Him, vision is ignited by the flame of passion. You start to know Him as a friend. An intuitive understanding of each other flourishes in the seedbed of love. Friends can feel when another friend is happy, grieved, or offended. Those deep feelings for the Holy Spirit keep me in the place of my first love, so I don't stray. The Holy Spirit's opinion trumps man's views, and that is the way it should be.

From intimacy with Him, I learn to hear the rhythms of His heart. I realize the more I get to know Him, the more I understand the direction where He wants to take me. I don't have to rely on what other men hear from the Lord for me. Instead, I arrive at an understanding of where the Lord wants to lead me, and then I allow others to speak into my life as voices of confirmation.

There are multitudes in the Body of Christ who have not learned this relationship with the Holy Spirit, but that is about to change. There is a new breed arising! This band of believers will cultivate an intimate relationship with the Holy Spirit and will not fall prey to men's control with selfish ambitions.

As we are infused with God's glory, we discover our old nature diminishing. Fear, anxiety, torment, depression, and panic disintegrate as God's power works in you. This is the day when God's people, full of power and love, lose their reputation and encounter a release of raw power and glory in the streets.

I recently had a dream, and in the dream, I was riding a motorcycle on the highways of America. Whenever I ride a motorcycle in my dreams, for me, it represents the ministry of the Holy Spirit. In the dream, I depended on men to tell me where I was going.

Instead of allowing the Holy Spirit to lead me, I kept stopping and asking directions from men. The more I did that, the more lost I became. I lost time by stopping and asking for directions. I sensed the Lord say, "People will experience acceleration in the glory, at this hour, by intimacy with the Holy Spirit." They won't waste time stopping and asking directions from men's traditions but freely they will move with the wind.

"The wind blows where it wants and you hear the sound of it, but you don't know where the wind comes from or where it is going. It is the same with every person who is born from the Spirit" (John 3:8).

We will be fully possessed and controlled by the Holy Spirit. We will hear His "sound" in our spirit, and know it is time to spread our wings and fly where He takes us. Then, we become a people pliable, ready to bring authentic revival.

In the dream, I met another problem; I was not prepared for the journey. I did not bring enough money to pay the toll booths. I feel like this represented being prepared in the spirit to advance in the kingdom, without delay. Jesus was a storyteller, and in the Gospel stories, he told ten short stories describing the kingdom. One of those stories was the parable of the ten virgins. *"Then the kingdom of heaven shall be likened to ten virgins who took their lamps and went out to meet the bridegroom. Now five of them were wise, and five were foolish"* (Mathew 25:1, 2). The bride of Christ is the church in her collective unity, and the juxtaposed characters are the members of the church, represented here by the ten virgins who were invited guests. Five of the virgins were portrayed as wise, whereas five were foolish. They were not depicted as bad or good, but imprudent and prudent, inattentive and thoughtful, unprepared and prepared.

The meaning behind the story is multi-faceted with lots of questions about the interpretation of the parable. Why virgins? What are the lamps the virgins carry? What is the oil? Who sells the oil? How do you buy it? Why is having enough oil the criterion for entrance through the door? It would take a whole book to drill down into the assorted layers of the parable.

Hidden in the words of Jesus are clues to these questions. For instance, Mathew 6:19, 20 provides a key. "Lay up for yourselves treasures in heaven." Jesus plays off the idea of preparation by investing in spiritual capital. The spiritual capital is illustrated in showing mercy to the poor, reaching out to the lost, preaching the gospel, acts of kindness and compassion. Be merciful as your Father in heaven is merciful (Luke 6:36). Preparation is not to be something guided by fear, but by wisdom. Many people are walking around, letting the present circumstances dictate their faith and expectations, rather than first seeking the kingdom of God.

It is essential that we recognize we are called to subdue the earth according to the creation mandate given to Adam. "*God blessed them and said to them, Be fruitful and multiply, and fill the earth and subdue it; rule over the fish of the sea and the birds of the air and every creature that crawls upon the earth*" (Genesis 1:28). Lack of resources is never a problem for a kingdom-minded person.

Lastly, in the dream, I finally got back on the right track. However, I noticed I was headed towards a bad part of town where drugs thrived, gangs lived, and violence was everywhere.

No problem. This is the culture where God loves to change people. Instead of riding through the inner-city neighborhood, with confidence and trust in the Lord, out of fear, I tried to escape. It is my constant prayer that the Holy Spirit will obliterate the fear of man.

The love warriors are arising. God is raising a new breed of dread champions in America and the nations. Desperate for the things of God, the champions' hearts are infatuated with the Holy Spirit. Many in this company of dread champions will be Latin Americans. Out of sheer love for God, we will manifest to America and to the nations the glory of His fame and the ever-present kingdom of power and glory.

I hope my vision inspires and ignites you. I invite you to become infected with the contagious love of our Lord. Come be a part of the dream team. Let's start dreaming bigger as we change our communities, bringing restoration for the Lord Jesus Christ. It is reformation time! While I don't endorse the seven cultural mountains of society teachings or victorious eschatology, I believe it will get very dark before Jesus returns, but I believe we will see the greatest harvest of humanity the world has ever seen.

8

THE DELICIOUS FRUIT OF THE SPIRIT

Before I can tell my life what I want to do with it, I must listen to my life telling me who I am.[1]

IN OUR SOCIETY, WE INCREASINGLY END UP BEING HUMAN DOINGS rather than human beings. The world tells us that what we achieve and accomplish in this life determines who we are, but the message of Jesus emphasizes who we should be, rather than what we do. The dynamics of life should be inside-out rather than outside-in.

Our culture is the busyness that branches out from where we define ourselves in terms of successes and possessions. As Walker Percy observed in his novel *Lancelot*, "To live in the past and future is easy. To live in the present is like threading a needle."

Longshoreman philosopher Eric Hoffer wrote, "We are warned not to waste time, but we are taught to waste our lives." This is evident in the tragedy of people who, in the first half of life, spend their health looking for wealth, and in the last half spend their wealth looking for health.[2]

Then some live life as it comes, without warning, like an actor going on stage unprepared. What value is our life if the first rehearsal for life is life itself? For many, life is like an outline because it is a summary without the details. Life pulls them into the dark circle of the fictive, naive, idealistic, and feigned romanticism.

In his book *Yes to Life*, Viktor Frankl accentuates my point. "A human being should never become a means to an end." Friedrich Hebbel closes the case with these words. "Life is not something; it is the opportunity for something."[3]

Being and doing are obviously necessary and interconnected, but the order is essential. What we do must emanate from who we are. Life should never be boring. A spark of life created by the Holy Spirit lights up the path before you, a path leading to self-discovery.

Throughout the Gospels, Jesus teaches the people, employing the power of stories to enable them to understand the kingdom. But he also asked questions. In fact, he asked a lot of questions. Actually, he asked 307 questions. His questions challenged religious leaders and disquieted the seeking soul. Like an oil rig drilling into hard soil, he cuts into the core of the human heart.

Then Jesus turned, and seeing them following, said to them, "What do you seek?" (John 1:38). The question is deliberate and direct. As Rudolf Bultmann wisely wrote, "It is clearly the first question that must be addressed to anyone who comes to Jesus, the first thing that must be clear."[4] This question escorts the two followers to a profound awareness of themselves, coming to understand who they are and what they are to become, as unveiled in their deepest desires.

SURRENDER!

The only thing you must do right now is to give up. It's time to fully surrender to the unfailing grace of the Lord Jesus Christ in your life. Life is always *now*, in this present moment. When you are in the present moment, you are not distracted by other things. Surrender your life to God, not the past or future, or your life situation. Lose the works of the flesh and eat life!

When most people hear the word *surrender*, they think of something negative. In a spiritual context, *surrender* means to let go of everything that disrupts and destroys and then to embrace what brings love, joy, and peace through Jesus. The endless circle of grace is surrender, acceptance, and reconciliation. Allow grace to produce its perfect work in you, again and again.

Your struggle is over, and your dreams are about to be released!

> Wherever you are
> Whatever you've been going through
> God says the struggle is over for you
> You've been in this place long enough
> And your mountainside has been rough
> The struggle is over for you[5]

Once upon a time, I was in a dream. I was standing over a pool of gorgeous waters. The light shined upwards into the atmosphere. It was on everything and was all around me. In this dream, the Lord spoke to me through a minister in my family. My heart was awakened to the mysteries and depths of Christ's unfailing love. I could feel my heart burning within me when He announced with compassion and abandonment, "I want to tell you the answer to EVERYTHING."

Pause and reflect on those words! How many of you would like to know the answer to everything? I know I would, and I am quite sure you would also.

Back to the dream. Jesus said, "What I have done on the cross through My blood is the absolute answer to everything. All you have to do is constantly yield to it by My grace."

I woke from the vision with a renewed sense of discovery and a need to run to Paul's epistles. In this season of my life, I anxiously desired to recover no other revelation but the delightful disclosure of God's grace through our Lord Jesus Christ.

Since that encounter, I took a deep dive into the Scriptures, studying the letters of Paul. I have been overwhelmed by fresh insight concerning our heavenly identity in Christ. I have heard many in the Body, saying God is bringing them back to that place of identity. You were placed in a divine witness program when your old life was expunged, crucified, and buried, never to be found again. You have been given a new identity in Jesus.

DOING BEGINS WITH BEING

Sad to write this, but it is true. His saints are struggling with frustrations originating with the feeling of not doing enough to please God. God would rather you first understand how it is enough by just being. Too many get lost spinning around in the

THE DELICIOUS FRUIT OF THE SPIRIT • 91

vortex of "being" versus "doing." You can't have one without the other. However, the order of priority is everything. Being comes before doing. If we focus on the "being," the "doing" would seem effortless. I know it sounds crazy but let me explain it by way of Christ's victory on the cross, and the Spirit's inner work.

When God looks for fruit, He doesn't look at a person's legalistic, religious efforts or slaving to prove your works' identity. In other words, He doesn't look at the "doing, doing, doing." This anxiety over work reminds me of the seven dwarfs' song, "Hi ho, hi ho it's off to work we go."

"You will know them by their fruits" (Matthew 7:16). It does not mean that he is unaware of our works, for Jesus said, *"I know your works,"* (Revelation 2:2). For clarity's sake, it does not mean he knows us by our works. He knows us for who we are in Him, by our fruits of the Spirit.

FRUITS VERSUS GIFTS

Don't confuse your identity with your gift. Gifts are given according to the Giver and are utilized in the capacity of serving others. The fruit grows gradually from the inside, whereas gifts come all at once from an outer source. We are not known in Heaven for what we do but for who we are. For example, in Heaven, we are not known as deliverance ministers or performers of signs or good works. We are known by our fruit.

It is critical to your spiritual health that you acknowledge and apprehend your identity. In this verse, Jesus adds a splash of color to the identity picture. *"Nevertheless, do not rejoice in this, that the spirits are subject to you, but rather rejoice because your names are written in heaven"* (Luke 10:20). The disciples were ecstatic about receiving the gift of power over the demonic enemies. But as power over demons can be intoxicating, the exercise of power must be tempered with humility. It is necessary that your primary joy is founded upon 'being' a kingdom citizen, approved by God. So, Jesus told them they should rejoice because their names are written in Heaven, and not because demons listened to them in His name.

This is massive proof that the Lord is more concerned about His Kingdom becoming an inner work in you than He is about it being demonstrated in an outer work, though both are amazing and crucial! The inner work of the Holy Spirit in the disciple's souls has greater value for Christ, than the outward works. They did not know yet, but they will soon know about the cross' power to transform them into His image.

We have discovered everything when we see our kingdom identity as an inward work, more than an outward power. "*Seeing that His divine power has granted to us everything pertaining to life and godliness, through the true knowledge of Him who called us by His own glory and excellence*" (I Peter: 1:3).

It all begins with grace. His gifts that flow through us are by grace alone. By grace, we are graciously able to steward our gifts, but they are not who we are. The exercise of the gifts points the world towards Christ, and not you.

CAN'T YOU TALK LOUDER, GOD?

"But the fruit of the Spirit is love, joy, peace, longsuffering, gentleness, goodness, faith, meekness, temperance: *against such there is no law*" (Galatians 5:22, 23).

Our heavenly identity is an inner working of the Holy Spirit, and it does not reach fruition until we fully surrender ourselves to His grace. For example, when joy, one of the Spirit's fruits, is fully mature, Father recognizes you as one of His sons. The Father knows you by your joy because of Christ's completed work on the cross in your life. But you must remember that joy isn't a work we do; it is the Holy Spirit's work in us. It just takes full surrender. That should lift the burden off of you.

It was New York City in the 1980s that Hank Martin and Archie Jordan wrote and recorded this poignant song, *To Be Victorious*.

To be victorious, you must surrender, surrender
completely to Me;
To be victorious, you must surrender, and I will set you
free;
I still can part the sea; the victory is in Me.

Do not be deceived that when God manifests His power in our lives, we can continue to live however we want. For example, a minister can enjoy God working in their life through miracles and then slowly begin to imagine that God validates a lifestyle of sin because God does miracles through them.

Let me be clear, the Lord is merciful, and His gifts are without repentance. He moves through people because He loves them. Souls are the business of Heaven. But if we are in sin, just because He acts through us, does not mean He validates our rebellion. He still wants purity to be combined with the gifts of the Holy Spirit, as we yield our lives to Him. When His fruit is manifested in us, then the law has no power over us.

With these words, Jesus strikes a dagger in the heart of those who use gifts to shelter them from rebellion. "Many will say to Me in that day, *'Lord, Lord, have we not prophesied in Your name, cast out demons in Your name, and done many wonders in Your name?' And then I will declare to them, 'I never knew you; depart from Me, you who practice lawlessness!'"* (Matthew 7:22, 23). Because they leaped over the fruit and went directly to the gifts, they never matured enough through the inner working of the Spirit, and thus they concocted a false identity. Because they elevated the gifts and disregarded the fruit, and by doing so, they created a lie by disregarding the life of sin they were living.

They longed for the Lord's approval based on what they did when it had nothing to do with it in the first place. It has everything to do with Jesus. Trying to get the Lord's approval through the law and continuing in defeat and sin, misses Christ's whole point. In Christ, you will experience all the acceptance you ever craved.

They hid sin in their lives, even with all their beautiful efforts. You might as well try climbing up to Heaven on a string of dental floss. His grace alone is what saves us and makes us a new creation. Everything boils down to who will ultimately yield their life to Jesus. Daily repentance is the single key! Rejoicing in Jesus and giving Him all the glory takes precedent.

I am reminded again of Christ's admonishment: Don't rejoice because demons listen to you in My name but rejoice in your eternal salvation. I sense the Lord bringing us back to that joyful place of blessed assurance in Him. If there is iniquity in your life, you can lay it down right now, making no more excuses. *He is faithful to forgive you right now and cleanse you of all unrighteousness!* (1 John 1:9). Isn't that good news! You can't do it in your strength. You have to do it in the power of Another, by merely surrendering to Him. Jesus can make the difference! When we learn how to yield to Jesus and to obey His teachings, we learn how to yield to loving Jesus and others.

I can't forget what the Lord showed Prophet Bob Jones in 1975 when he died of a heart attack, went to Heaven, and then returned to life. Bob said one amazing thing. In his encounter in Heaven, he was standing in a line of people before the Lord, and, to each person standing in from of Him, He asked them one question: "Did you learn how to love?" He didn't ask, "Did you learn how to prophesy or heal the sick?"

Those are all gifts that operate as an outer function of the Lord's goodness. But the new creation reality makes it clear that the Kingdom of God is an inward work that makes us loving where we were once hateful, joyful when we were once depressed, forgiving when we were once bitter, and the list goes on. When we take credit for something that is a byproduct of being a believer, we are dangerously in error.

THE ACE UP GOD'S SLEEVE

John 15:5-8 is the ace up God's sleeve. *"If we abide in Him and let His words abide in us, we will bear much fruit. By this, we will show ourselves to be His disciples."* While we desperately need power in the church and miracles that demonstrate His goodness, there must be more. *"By this all men will know that you are My disciples, if you have love for one another"* (John 13:35).

As the world gets darker, the church is shining brighter! This is an amazing season of the Lord bearing fruit that will remain in our lives through simply knowing Christ crucified and risen again. "And the glory of the LORD shall be revealed, and all flesh shall see it together: for the mouth of the LORD hath spoken it" (Isaiah 40:5)

Lord, I thank You that in this season, You are restoring our true heavenly identity in the simplicity of Christ, and by knowing this simple truth, we will know the truth all over again, and the truth will set us free! Amen and amen!

9

EXCHANGING LIFELESS CHRISTIANITY FOR POWER

The reason the world is not seeing Jesus is that Christian people are not filled with Jesus. They are satisfied with attending meetings weekly, reading the Bible occasionally, and praying sometimes. It is an awful thing for me to see people who profess to be Christians lifeless., powerless, and in a place where their lives are so parallel to unbelievers' lives that it is difficult to tell which place they are in, whether in the flesh or in the spirit. (Smith Wigglesworth)[1]

CROATIAN BORN PHYSICIST AND JESUIT PRIEST, JOSEPH Boscovitch, discovered that an atom is a mere center of force. The electrons of an atom are attracted to the protons in an atomic nucleus by the electromagnetic force. The protons and neutrons in the nucleus are attracted to each other by the nuclear force.[2]

When scientists analyze its elementary components, they see it is alive with energies inconceivably subtle. All this force is the immediate power of the omnipotent and omnipresent Creator.

The failure with many Christians is they have taken too low an estimate of their present position and spiritual potential. It is time to trade your lifeless Christianity for God's power.

The Gospel is to be presented, not as a lifeless theory, but as a living force to empower life and change the world. One of the reasons Christianity is often lifeless is, we unconsciously remove our life experiences from our faith. We are content to talk about God or to listen to someone talk about him once a week. Without God's authority and power, words are lifeless.

We are like a harp constructed of many strings responding to the heavenly music created by the fingers of God. The touch of the Master's fingers will awaken the gifts and powers within you.

REVITALIZED BY THE LIFE WITHIN

Sadly, too many live unaware of the potent energies dwelling with us, inhabiting and empowering us with a supernatural life force within. When we meet someone, instinctively, we know they are different. It isn't because of what they wear or how they talk. It has nothing to do with the religious badge they wear or the code to which they adhere. It is that they know Jesus, and that made the difference. They dwell in him, and he dwells in them. He is the power for their walk and the source of life, and it is revealed in everything they do.

Praise be to the God and Father of our Lord Jesus Christ, who has blessed us in the heavenly realms with every spiritual blessing in Christ. For he chose us in him before the creation of the world to be holy and blameless in his sight (Ephesian 1:3, 4). "*The peace of Christ rules in your hearts*" (Colossians 3:15). "*The power of Christ is made perfect in their weakness*" (2 Corinthians 12:9).

"*The life of Christ is made manifest in their mortal flesh*" (2 Corinthians 4:11).

The expressions "in Christ," "in the Lord," and "in him" occur 164 times in the letters of Paul alone, and are indispensable to an understanding of the New Testament. John Stott frames a beautiful picture of life in Christ. "To be "in Christ" does not mean to be inside Him. It is not like tools in a box, or clothes in a closet. It is to be organically united to Christ, as a limb is in the body or a branch is in the tree. It is this personal relationship with Christ that is the distinctive mark of his authentic followers."[3]

Those who embrace the power of the Christ life experience serenity which adversity cannot pickpocket, a spiritual power that weakness cannot extinguish, and an energy of life that cannot be asphyxiated.

IN HIM, WE LIVE, MOVE, AND HAVE OUR BEING

For in him we live, and move, and have our being; as certain also of your own poets have said, For we are also his offspring (Acts 17:28).

Like an author who borrows a quote from a song, the Apostle Paul was comfortable in quoting a didactic poem written by the Greek poet, Aratus, who was a countryman of the Apostle Paul. Arastus' quotation opens with an invocation to Zeus, which Paul confiscates and uses for his own unique purpose.

Flattery was not his purpose. He uses this Greek quote to *preach against* Greek culture, underlining its absurdities. He is not vindicating the latent wisdom of the Greeks; he is exposing their foolish inconsistencies. From Paul's lips, the quote is repossessed and pressed into a kingdom truth.

Unfortunately, too many in the body of Christ live unaware of their latent power and the potential made possible by the life of God within us.

To extract the meaning of Paul's words, we lean into the depth of the meaning of live, move, and have our being. Christ is the original fountain of life, and he upholds us in the marvel of each moment. Paul traces our dependence on Jesus from the lowest rhythm of life to the highest powers of action and regenerated existence. It would be impossible to express in more explicit language the importance of our total dependence On God.

J.W. Whiton paints a mural accurately exhibiting the essence of Paul's words. "This the processes of growth and repair are carried on unrestingly by this same chemical energy of God ever gluing atom to atom in blood, skin, and bone, etc., under the direction of the master workman we call Life, in whose skill we see the Divine intelligence of Him in whom we live and who renews our substance day by day.

"The word 'move' does not refer to the motion of persons from place to place, but to those internal movements of the mind and spirit of which the outward actions are the effect. St Paul means that the feelings of men are acted on by God, who speaks to the heart. It means that we derive strength to move from him; an expression denoting "constant and absolute dependence." There is no idea of dependence more striking than that we owe to him the ability to perform the slightest motion. So, again with our instincts; their automatic power is the immediate energy of the God in whom we live."[4]

"We are His offspring." We didn't come by some evolutionary process or some cosmic form, but we are the offspring of God. His stream of life fills the tiny pools of our existence. Our thoughts spring God's thoughts. Our discoveries are His revelations. We pray, but prayer is the circulation of His Spirit praying through us and to Him again. As God's offspring, we must stand in oneness with God, forever remaining in indispensable connection with Him. Only in Him do we have life and life more abundantly.

BELIEVE IN HIM WHOM HE HAS SENT

When Jesus was asked how do we do the works of the Father, He replied with a simple but profound revelation found in John 6:29, "*Jesus answered and said to them, 'This is the work of God, that you should believe in Him whom He has sent.'*"

If you are a Spirit-filled believer, washed by the blood of Jesus, all you have to do is believe in the Son of God. To believe is to trust and to place full confidence in Christ, yielding the will and affections, accompanied by humble dependency on Him.

Signs follow the believer, as revealed in Mark 16:17-18. "*And these signs shall follow them that believe; in My name shall they cast out devils; they shall speak with new tongues; they shall take up serpents; and if they drink any deadly thing, it shall not hurt them; they shall lay hands on the sick, and they shall recover.*"

To distinguish ourselves from the world and display the mark of a Christian, we must lose all doubt and unbelief and go upside down. Humble yourself and believe the Gospel. All pride and fear of man must be thrown out the window. *"If you believe, you will see the glory of God"* (John 11:40). Jesus made it clear that the mixture of prayer and belief create an environment for answered prayer. *"Whatsoever things you desire when you pray, believing, you shall receive them, and you shall have them"* (Mark 11:24).

It's not our job to heal the sick, it's only our job to act and believe in Jesus. The more we pray for the sick, those in need of miracles, and those tormented by evil spirits, the more God will trust us with increased healing power. Each act of faith will usher in the great last days' harvest of souls. Steward His gifts for His glory and His fame alone!

God's power activates the imagination, causing you to reflect beyond your wildest thought. *"Now to the one who can do infinitely more than all we can ask or imagine according to the power that is working among us."* (Ephesians 3:20, ESV).

HOSTING HIS PRESENCE

When you imagine with God, it catapults you to a place where you no longer pursue His presence, but you become a host for His presence. You discover a realm where nothing is impossible. In revival meetings and at churches, Jennifer and I often see God do creative miracles in the glory realm, without even touching the people. Sometimes, some of the coolest miracles I've seen God do are imagining them occur before they happen! It's like I dreamed by faith at the moment, and God performed it.

People have received vision miracles, saw eardrums restored, and new teeth planted, without anyone touching them while they were in the atmosphere of praise, worship, and decree. We have seen God dissolve metal in people's bodies, some that had been there for over 25 years. We witnessed God extend limbs, scars vanish, tumors disappear, people receiving a gold crown and new teeth, and stage four cancers obliterated by God's power, and so much more. Many of these miracles were doctor-verified, before and after x-rays.

When these things happen in our midst, we watch many come to receive Christ as Savior, including people from other religions and cults. Since 2000, God sent my wife and me to thirty nations, and we lived in Israel for a year, observing and enjoying the amazing exploits done to bring glory to Jesus. These miracles resulted in people being saved! Healing is definitely my assignment! It is not just for me. You can operate in this harvest glory; also, with your assignment, bring people to Christ!

It is amazing how many people we saw healed, even through social networking, live streaming, and even cell phone calls, while conducting meetings. I believe it will happen to you if you need healing, even while reading this book!

GOD, CAN'T YOU TALK LOUDER?

Once, while on hosting a live streaming event, we saw a miracle. I mentioned a woman's name online and described her physical condition caused by a car accident (this accident was in the 1980s and caused whiplash in her neck), and I told her exactly where it was hurting, all through a word of knowledge. I released the power of God over her during the live broadcast. While she was on live stream, she said she felt fire touch her and was completely healed. No longer did she have the pain caused by a thirty-year-old ailment!

A SWEEPING OF MIGHTY MIRACLES

God can move through us, accompanied by extraordinary miracles, even when the ones we are praying for are not present. During a meeting in Brazil, I simply laid my hand on a picture a lady brought me of a man who had been in a coma for eight months. At the minute I prayed over his picture, he got up and called her to report that Jesus healed him! Imagine that! These stories are not designed to create fans, but they are designed to inspire you to become participants in Jesus' glory and fame.

These are the days when the Holy Spirit sets many people free from passive Christianity, unaware of their complacency. We will never arrive at a release of the supernatural Kingdom culture unless each believer is introduced to the importance of biblical teaching and personal discipline. We must challenge and awaken the body of Christ from their sleeping slumber, creating an awakening that will lead to doing the greater works Jesus promised to those who believe.

The Bible has much to say about healing. Here are some Scriptures that will increase your faith to go forward, in His name, and heal the sick. These Scriptures refer to the healing ministry of Jesus.

THE BASIS OF HEALING IS JESUS' WORK ON THE CROSS

It is God's nature to heal, as revealed through Jesus.

"And Jesus went about all Galilee, teaching in their synagogues, preaching the Gospel of the kingdom, and healing all kinds of sickness and all kinds of disease among the people. Then His fame went throughout all Syria; and they brought to Him all sick people who were afflicted with various diseases and torments, and those who were demon-possessed, epileptics, and paralytics; and He healed them" (Mt. 4:23-24).

"Then Jesus went about all the cities and villages, teaching in their synagogues, preaching the gospel of the kingdom, and healing every sickness and every disease among the people" (Mt. 9:35).

"And great multitudes followed Him, and He healed them all" (Mt. 12:15).

"And the whole multitude sought to touch Him, for power went out from Him and healed them all" (Lk. 6:19).

These verses are only a sampling of the healing power of Jesus, as seen in the Gospel stories. For more look up the following verses.

Matthew 4:23-24; 8:16-17; 9:35; 10:8; 11:5-6; 12:15-17; 14:14, 34-36; 15:30-31; 19:1-2; 21:14; Mark 1:32-34, 39, 45; 3:10; 6:5-6; 6:53-57; Luke 4:40; 5:15; 6:17-19; 7:21-23; 9:1-2, 6; 10:1, 9, 19; John 2:23; 9:6-7; 11:43-45; 14:12

Jesus purchased our healing on the cross. One of the reasons He came was to destroy the work of Satan.

"When evening had come, they brought to Him many who were demon-possessed. And He cast out the spirits with a word, and healed all who were sick, that it might be fulfilled which was spoken by Isaiah the prophet, saying: "He Himself took our infirmities And bore our sicknesses" (Mt. 8:16-17).

"God anointed Jesus of Nazareth with the Holy Spirit and with power, who went about doing good and healing all who were oppressed by the devil, for God was with Him" (Acts 10:38).

"For this purpose, the Son of God was manifested that He might destroy the works of the devil" (1 Jn. 3:8).

THE POWER TO HEAL IS PROMISED IN THE NEW TESTAMENT

Every believer can operate in the healing anointing in the name of Jesus!

"And as you go, preach, saying, 'The Kingdom of Heaven is at hand. Heal the sick, cleanse the lepers, raise the dead, cast out demons. Freely you have received, freely give'" (Matthew 10:7-8).

"And heal the sick there, and say to them, 'The kingdom of God has come near to you.'" "Then the seventy returned with joy, saying, 'Lord, even the demons are subject to us in Your name.'" "He said to them... 'Behold I give you the authority to trample on serpents and scorpions, and over all the power of the enemy, and nothing shall by any means hurt you'" (Luke 10:9-19).

"And these signs will follow those who believe: In My name they will cast out demons... they will lay hands on the sick, and they will recover" (Mark. 16:17-18).

"Most assuredly, I say to you, he who believes in Me, the works that I do he will do also; and greater works than these he will do, because I go to My Father" (John. 14:12).

"Is anyone among you sick? Let him call for the elders of the church and let them pray over him and anoint them with oil in the name of the Lord. The prayer of faith will save the sick, and the Lord will raise him up" (James. 5:14-15).

Believers healed the sick in the early Church

"Through the hands of the apostles many signs and wonders were done among the people... so that they brought the sick out into the streets and laid them on beds and couches, that at least the shadow of Peter passing by might fall on some of them. Also, a multitude gathered from the surrounding cities to Jerusalem, bringing sick people and those who were tormented by unclean spirits, and they were all healed" (Acts 5:12-16).

"Philip went down to the city of Samaria and preached Christ to them... For unclean spirits, crying with a loud voice, came out of many who were possessed; and many who were paralyzed, and lame were healed. And there was great joy in that city" (Acts 8:5-8).

"Now God worked unusual miracles by the hands of Paul, so that even handkerchiefs or aprons were brought from his body to the sick, and the diseases left them, and the evil spirits went out of them... So, the Word of the Lord grew mightily and prevailed." (Acts 19:11-20)

For more look up the following verses. Acts 2:43; 4:33; 5:12-16; 8:18; 9:38; 19:11-12

10

A NEW ERA IN THE BODY OF CHRIST

"BEHOLD! I am doing a new thing." He is calling us to come up and out of the ordinary and rise above our limits. He is asking us to SEE and RESPOND to His hand of preparation and purpose in our lives and in the Church - His Bride. To behold what He has done, is doing and will continue to do as we live righteously, according to the Word of God and with a vision to see His kingdom come here on earth. [1]

FIFTY DAYS AFTER THE RESURRECTION OF JESUS AND TEN DAYS after he ascended into Heaven, an event of epic proportions took place, shifting the course of history. One hundred and twenty disciples were huddled in Jerusalem, waiting for God's power to descend or for armed soldiers to break down the doors. The day of Pentecost was the day on which the Holy Spirit made a unique visit to earth. The Pentecost fire fell, tongues of fire leaped from each one's head, and they were filled with the Holy Spirit.

The uproar surrounding Pentecost didn't go unnoticed.

Rumors began spreading through the streets of Jerusalem, and crowds started gathering in the area, just west of the temple complex. At some point, Peter stood up in front of the growing crowds, and with newly found boldness, he raised his voice and addressed the curious crowd. When he was finished, 3,000 people accepted his message and were baptized that day. From 120 disciples in hiding to a movement of over 3,000 Jesus followers in just one day. It was the beginning of a new era.

The first Christians were revolutionaries. The group they formed was, in many ways, very different from what we know as the church today. According to the Book of Acts, they met in their homes and devoted themselves to God's Word. As a result, these early Christians initiated the most amazing and powerful transformation the world has ever known. Christians emerged amid an enormously diverse Roman melting pot of social and religious ideas. They completely changed the Empire and united it under the banner of Christ.

Early Christians did not *go* to church, they *were* the church; they impacted their culture as the people of God. In those glorious days, the church was marinating in the supernatural, soaking in God's presence, pressing into the kingdom, manifesting the love of God, increasing in numbers, and preaching the gospel in all the world.

Behind every miracle, there was a force that drove God's purposes and pulsated with divine energy. Without that power, the apostles become ordinary men; with that power, they changed the world.

Pagan powers were broken, the lame healed, the dead raised from the dead, and thousands of souls were born again. Never before were men possessed with such passion for speaking out for Christ. Never before had there been such a willingness to suffer for Christ. Never before had a group so large experienced such zeal and intimate fellowship. The world was standing on the sidelines, watching this new thing. Eventually, their witness in Jerusalem branched out to Judea and Samaria, and then pushed their way to the uttermost part of the earth. This was the age of the Spirit, who came to abide with them.

In Acts 2:42-47, Luke reveals the secret to the church's life and power catapulting them to the ends of the earth. *"And they devoted themselves to the apostles' teaching and the fellowship, to the breaking of bread and the prayers. And awe came upon every soul, and many wonders and signs were being done through the apostles. And all who believed were together and had all things in common. And they were selling their possessions and belongings and distributing the proceeds to all, as any had need. And day by day, attending the temple together and breaking bread in their homes, they received their food with glad and generous hearts, praising God and having favor with all the people. And the Lord added to their number day by day those who were being saved.*

A LIFE INSCRIBED WITH GLORY

We are entering a new era in the Body of Christ, and we will see the prophetic fulfillment of 'living epistles' being released to the nations. Pentecost is a planned event. It is no mere afterthought with God. The church is being reformed and anointed by God's eternal presence and spiritual power. Pentecost was the guarantee of the presence of the Holy Spirit. He came to indwell and possess the hearts of men and women.

God is about to release a corporate revelation to His church, while He calls us to arise and shine, full of the Word and the Spirit, whose lives men will read, and their lives will be transformed.

"Ye are our epistle written in our hearts, known and read of all men: forasmuch as ye are manifestly declared to be the epistle of Christ ministered by us, written not with ink, but with the Spirit of the Living God; not in tables of stone, but fleshy tables of the heart (2 Corinthians 3:2, 3). The signature of sin, written on men's hearts, is erased and eradicated by Christ, and a new inscription is indelibly inscribed on their hearts. This "writing" is not written with ink on a papyrus roll but is the mystical imprint of the Holy Spirit on their hearts, transparent for all to read.

People will be able to read you! Demons will recognize you and be petrified if you are a believer. You are a heavenly Xerox copy, embossed by the fingers of God and engraved with His image. You walk on the earth with God's DNA, as God's nature is displayed in your life. Jesus died and purchased a family who reflects Him in the earth and when Christ appears, then you will appear with Him in glory (see Colossians 3:4).

That is not a promise you are waiting on; it has already happened if you believe! In other words, you are already glorified. We appear with Him in glory, as we release the glory on the earth! *"Whereunto he called you by our gospel, to the obtaining of the glory of our Lord Jesus Christ"* (2 Thessalonians 2:14). The glory God gave Jesus, He has shared with us that we be partakers of that glory. *"And the glory which You gave Me I have given them, that they may be one just as We are one"* (John 17:22).

Romans 8:30 accentuates this truth. *"Moreover whom He did predestinate, them He also called: and whom He called, them He also justified: and whom He justified, them He also glorified."*

I once made a joke while my good friend was preaching on justification. I said, "We are eternally on 'Just-a-vacation'" – a play on words of 'justification' from dead works. It's just an easy vacation while you slippity slip when you "wallkety walk" because your tracks are dripping with butterfat. *"Thou hast crowned the year of Thy goodness, And Thy paths drop fatness. We are dead to dead works and we have lost them"* (Psalms 65:11).

"If then you be dead with Christ from the elements of this world, why do you yet decree as though living in the world? Touch not, taste not, handle not: Which all are unto destruction by the very use, according to the precepts and doctrines of men. Which things have indeed a shew of wisdom in superstition and humility, and not sparing the body, not in any honor to the filling of the flesh?" See Colossians 2:20-23, Douay-Rheims 1899 American Edition.

PEOPLE CAN READ US

Evangelism will take a new direction as we father sons and daughters in the faith. That will drive the church into new places "until we all attain to the unity of the faith, and of the knowledge of the Son of God, to a mature man, to the measure of the stature which belongs to the fullness of Christ" (See Ephesians 4:13). The Greek word Paul uses, *teleios*, has a special meaning. It implies "an end, a goal, a limit," and it combines dual ideas: first, the full development of one's powers; and second, the attainment of some goal or standard—the realization of the proper end of one's existence. As we mature, we become more powerful and compelling in our witness to the world.[2]

Maturity brings you to new levels of creativity in how you approach unbelievers. It isn't a theological shift but a transformational shift. We won't be merely urging people to say the sinner's prayer with lip service, but we will be pouring our lives into the ones we lead to Christ, with the goal of bringing them to maturity. Jesus' audience was the multitudes, but His ultimate goal was to train His disciples. By the process of multiplication, He would change the world.

It is time for the true fathers to arise, fathers who don't build for themselves, but help build leaders. A true leader does not gather a bunch of followers; they seek to build up a cluster of leaders.

God desires us to have a people whose radical love outshines the darkness. *"And the light shines in the darkness, and the darkness did not comprehend it"* (John 1:5). By the power of God, many will speak and stall or divert natural disasters, such as earthquakes and tornadoes. The forces of nature must listen to the voice of the Lord. Great fear will come upon the church as in the book of Acts, not terror, but awe of the love, grace, and power of the resurrected Lord Jesus Christ. *"So great fear came upon all the church and upon all who heard these things"* (Acts 5:11). The church was struck with a holy awe of God and his judgments, thrusting them into worship and thankfulness for God's mighty power.

I envision a day when believers will walk into schools and universities, full of God's glory, testifying of Jesus' love, and the power of the Holy Spirit. In that holy atmosphere, people will come under conviction of their dire need for Jesus. It will not be by works but by revealing who we are as God's living epistles. God will release creativity in how we present the gospel to people in this ever-changing society.

One of my favorite forms of evangelism is walking into a college classroom and sharing my testimony of how Jesus Christ saved me. It's the perfect atmosphere to capture people's attention. School cafeterias are also great places for evangelism. Using my partners' contributions, we are able to announce this message to the hundreds of people standing in line: "Whoever needs help buying lunch today, I'm standing at the checkout corner and I will pay for your meal." Next, we share with them the glorious gospel of Jesus; the reactions are absolutely priceless.

I believe we partner with angels when we're ministering the gospel to people on the streets. I remember when I went out on the streets and I perceived an angel standing next to me while ministering to a very broken girl who was bipolar. I told her to put her hand into the angel on my right side, while talking to her about the Kingdom of God. She did, and then screamed with joy as she felt this amazing energy of love touching her every time, she put her hand into the angel. She cried out, thanking the Lord Jesus Christ!

MASS YOUTH HARVEST

I have sensed God saying, "Ask Me for stadiums, arenas, civic centers, and more because I am going to fill them with young people." God says, "Chicago, you are Mine! New York City, you are Mine! Kiev Ukraine, you are Mine!" There will be more cities God is claiming for His kingdom. Young people will not be forced by their parents to go to the house of God because they will go by their own will. They will experience freedom from sin through what Jesus did for them. It will elevate them above stale religious sermons and churches who are blind, leading the blind.

Mercy is falling! Mercy is falling on the youth of America! God is calling forth a company of young people who will not fear death for the sake of the gospel. When we go to the streets and rough neighborhoods, we don't see the danger, we see Jesus! As we are filled with His love, we unplug from our self-generated works, and we plug into a life, super-charged with Jesus' power. We don't fear man, obstacles, or sacrificing our lives for the cross of Jesus. When you are so full of His glory, you can only love the world, as God does.

NO MORE TIMIDITY

I must brag on many of the African churches with whom I have relationships. I have ministered in small crusades in Uganda, Nigeria, Benin, and Togo, and there is a common thread in all the lives of the local believers; it is the shimmering shine reflected from them. They are driven by their faith in Jesus Christ, even in regions filled with darkness and witchcraft. The Africans' faith dazzle with boldness and I have seen names of businesses reflecting their faith, like this one, "Holy Ghost Auto Repairs."

WE ARE NOT OUT OF GAS

God will help Christians who relapsed back into a false belief system because they ran out of gas with the Holy Spirit! Wet blanket theology would have us believe that we must run to Heaven every time we need a refill because we have poured out so much on others. That is a poorly concocted spiritual equation. God never intended that each time we dry up we rush back to God for more, begging that He fills our empty gas tank with more of Him. We should live in the glory daily, without draining our tank. In contradiction to that weak approach to life, John wrote that God does not give the Spirit by measure (John 3:34). The Weymouth New Testament created an alternative approach to this verse. *"For He whom God has sent speaks God's words; for God does not give the Spirit with limitations."* Believe it and receive it!

A CHURCH THAT MAKES SENSE TO THE WORLD

The Lord spoke to my heart recently and said, "The world culture outside of church culture is changing fast. Many in the church forgot how to make Christ relevant in our times. I am raising a new breed of believers who will undergo a major shift in their mindset, and I remove the church from the shadows of timidity and fear and move them into the boldness of My Spirit."

God is not only a God of individuals and families, or a God of churches, but He wants to be a God of communities, a God of nations! "I am raising a community that will build people rather than tear them down. I will disassemble the backstabbing and backbiting that encounter influences in the prophetic streams. We will see a culture of honor released in the prophetic stream, the glory stream, and in all streams and denominations across the globe." In these spheres of honor, people will know we are His disciples because of the love we have for each another (John 13:35).

The Body of Christ is rising out of their false identities as they discover and embrace their true identity in Christ, and from that new view they will disciple nations! You are much bigger on the inside than you are on the outside! It's time for diverse people groups to come to Jesus. If God can do it in Iran, He can do it anywhere.

"God, I ask You to release a mass company of living epistles in the nations, full of faith, wisdom, power, and love, who will be fully read among the nations. May they make Your Kingdom be on earth as it is in Heaven, preparing the world for the second coming of the Lord Jesus Christ."

He is coming back for a glorious Bride, releasing boldness, authority, and Holy Spirit fun in Your church and in Your holy, precious name, let us shine Your light so bright amid the darkness! What amazing days we are living in!

"Fear not, little flock, for it has been the good pleasure of your Father to give you the Kingdom (Luke 12:32, Darby Translation)

JUICY FRUIT

WHAT PROOF DO WE HAVE THAT THIS HIDDEN AND ETHEREAL Spirit is active in our lives? If walking in the Spirit is the mark of the believer, what can we do to verify He is leading us? In the writings of the Apostle Paul, we find answers to the question.

"To each is given the manifestation of the Spirit for the common good. All these are empowered by one and the same Spirit, who apportions to each one individually as he wills" (1 Corinthians 12:7, 11, ESV).

"But the fruit of the Spirit is love, joy, peace, patience, kindness, goodness, faithfulness, gentleness, self-control; against such things there is no law" (Galatians 5:22, 23, ESV).

First, we must start in the Gospel of John. Jesus had been the Comforter of the disciples during His earthly sojourn, but now that He was going away to be with the Father, they needed someone to care for them as He had done. Instead of losing by His departure, they would gain; the Holy Spirit would empower them, gift them, care for them, and be the divine catalyst for spiritual growth.

The gifts of the Holy Spirit are more appealing to most Christians. Many seek the gifts, not as many pursue the fruit. Gifts are more instantaneous, while fruit takes longer to mature. The gifts of the Spirit are reflected in what we do, where the fruit of the Spirit are displayed in who we are. The gifts are the outward manifestation of the Spirit's work, while the fruit is an inward, invisible work of the Spirit. There's nothing flashy about the fruit. A gifted person has more appeal and magnetism because of their ministry and spiritual ability. For these reasons and perhaps others, the gifts of the Spirit receive far more attention in our culture, than does the fruit of the Spirit.

The fruit of the Spirit is sometimes doomed to obscurity, hidden in the shadow of the more preferred gifts. However, the fruit of the Spirit is the provision and protection for those walking in the Spirit, provisions for growth and protection from temptation.

Nevertheless, both are crucial to the Christian life, and neither should be minimized. The gifts of the Spirit are essential for building the body and influencing the world. The fruit of the Spirit is vital for our spiritual growth and as reflectors of the glory of God. In this chapter, I focus on juicy fruit.

The Christian life is a pilgrimage. As a biblical metaphor, the fruit of the Spirit is connected to life's journey and development. Walking in the Spirit is a relatively slow mode of transportation. Paul didn't say we fly in the Spirit or drive in the Spirit. We walk in the Spirit while leaping over obstacles and avoiding barriers in our journey towards maturity. At every point, we face the speed bumps of the flesh. All along life's journey, the spirit has given us the fruit of the Spirit to enable and encourage us to mature in the life God has given us.

In his letter to the church in Galatia, Paul introduced the topic of the fruit of the Spirit. One might have suspected that he made a mistake when he wrote fruit, instead of fruits of the Spirit. But it was no mistake, a mistake many have made over the years. He addressed it as a singular fruit. Alexander MacLaren, the biblical expositor, accurately addressed this issue. "All this rich variety of graces, of conduct and character, is thought of as one. The individual members are not isolated graces, but all connected, springing from one root and constituting an organic whole."[1]

The first of the three triads include love, joy, and peace. They are the results of communion with God and the indwelling of the Spirit. Love is at the top of the list because it is the foundation and moving principle of all the rest. It is the expression of the higher life, which is a love shed abroad in the heart by the Holy Spirit. It is the life sap that rises through the tree and gives form to all the clusters.

The remaining two members of this triad are the consequences of the first. In the first triad of fruit, the reality of the Holy Spirit's presence is disclosed in the depth of our love, the height of our joy, and the breadth of our peace. In the second triad of fruit, we will be tested but we will triumph through the patience of our long-suffering, the sweetness of kindness, and the delight of goodness. In the third and final triad of fruit, life is manifested in the longevity of faithfulness, the modesty of meekness, and the self-restraint of temperance.

THE SPIRIT OF GRACE AND OVERCOMING POWER

Much of what I write is simple enough for young and old to easily grasp. My writing focuses on the importance of reimagining our life. Subsequently, the understanding and the applications of it are life-transforming. Reimagining is a lifelong process. We must continually be engaged in the process while staying vital, fully alive in the present, and remaining hopeful for the future. As you travel through life, it is important that occasionally you reexamine where you are and refocus on where you are going. In reimaging your life, you must regularly ask yourself if your choices have been correct and have sustained you so far, or if wrong decisions or opposition from the dark side is weighing you down. At this time, there is a fresh release from the Father of abundant grace for the weary traveler!

There has been an onslaught of the enemy, attempting to steal vision from the sons and daughters of the living God. The hordes of hell's relentless attempts to infuse apathy in the heart of the Lord's bride will be disannulled by a Church arising with tears in their eyes for their Creator and moving with compassion towards lost souls who must yield to Him.

Has despair visited you in this past season due to discouragement, disappointment, and even fear of the unknown? I'm putting my faith in action with yours, so don't worry. Father God has an ace up His sleeve right now!

God is about to release the Spirit of grace to help you overcome! As this happens, the revelation of the finished work of the cross will ignite complete joy and liberty in you! The revelation of being dead to the flesh and alive in Christ will become so common for those set free by this death and life. God desires to fully eradicate the spirit of religion off people's lives. He is about to inject into His Church a passion for His Spirit, unlike any other time we have known in history.

So, let's go on a quick journey together and find the pathway into limitless life in the Spirit and the next great outpouring, reformation, and renaissance in the earth. A new zeal will come upon you to lift into the heights of God's glorious life designed for you through Christ Jesus. Don't throw the towel in now? The best is yet to come.

There are some airlines where flight attendants come down the aisle and offer passengers "duty -free" items. However, few people purchase these items, which I find to be somewhat parabolic. God is offering you His spiritual gifts, His spiritual fruit, and an eternal, blissful life transformed by Him. These are "duty-free" and "works-free." Today, you can receive all of God's life, provided for you and made accessible through Jesus' death on the cross, including His burial and resurrection.

God desires to transition Christ's body from head knowledge to experiential knowledge. In that process, God will continually fill you with the intoxicating presence and power of His Spirit.

HEAVEN AIRWAYS

Please allow me to be parabolically playful for just a moment. "Ladies and gentlemen, this is Your captain speaking! We want to thank you for flying Heaven Airways today. We are now soaring at a very high altitude over the mountains standing in your way as I remove your past ineffective foundations. The flight attendants will be coming down the aisle to offer you, your church, and your ministry, these 'duty-free' items. For those of you who have been serving the Lord, more out of duty and religious, unfulfilled service, you are about to be redirected, refreshed, and reignited by the Spirit of grace when you buy these items, without money and without cost (See Isaiah 55:1-2).

Sound fun? When you receive God's gift, you will be thrust into new favor in your ministry, life, business, or in whatever sphere God has for you. God wants a company of people to be fully enriched with His divine nature, supernatural power, and the fruit of the Spirit. Moving from this empowered position, you will go into the deep dark places of the world directly into the enemy's territory and then harvest humanity for the cause of Christ. At the appointed time of harvest, the farmer knows he must go into the fields to reap his crops; otherwise, his harvest would perish. *"Then He said to them, "The harvest truly is great, but the laborers are few; therefore, pray the Lord of the harvest to send out laborers into His harvest"* (Luke 10:2).

In Zechariah 12:10, the author declares that the Lord will pour out a Spirit of grace and supplication upon His people. Enabled by the Holy Spirit, a company of God's saints will enter into deep realms of prayer and supplication, asking the Lord to pour out His presence on the nations. It will take the Spirit of grace to go into the dark and treacherous places to reap the harvest prepared by God! He will make it fun! The enemy knows it is a time of great harvest in the earth and he has tried to stop you, but the God of supernatural peace and power is about to crush Satan under your feet (See Romans 16:20).

As you fully yield to the Helper, the Comforter, the Alongside One, then the Holy Spirit of God will begin to fulfill the promise to implement God's rule, dominion, and reign over the nations. Jesus emboldens and encourages the overcomers as they advance into the world, proclaiming Christ's victory. *"And he who overcomes, and keeps My works until the end, to him I will give power over the nations"* (Revelation 2:26).

Is that just for the consummation at the end of the age? No! It is for right now! Many of you reading this, who were tempted to retreat from battle, now are about to encounter a Holy Spirit intoxication. This is not to negate the fact that you are filled with the Holy Spirit, but simply that the Holy Spirit is about to possess you with new grace.

For those who drink the new wine of the Spirit, He will release and activate a supernatural advancement accompanied by fresh vision, a sense of renewed purpose, and faith that overcomes the world. As a result of dedicating yourself to this new realm of glory, like trances, third heaven encounters like Paul, transportations, translations, and other supernatural experiences will become more available and common.

Through these experiences, God's kingdom of power and glory deposited in your yearning heart will flow from you to the ends of the earth. New strategies will be given you, and a season of acceleration will come upon you. Many are saying, "Man, I have wasted so many years!" God trumps your burden of wasted years by saying, *"I understand, but I am helping you redeem the time you lost through a quick work I am about to do in you!"* The prophet Joel prophesied it into existence. *"I will restore the years that the locust has eaten"* (Joel 2:25).

INTOXICATED WITH GOD AND NUMB TO THE CARES OF THIS WORLD

In the parable of the sower, Jesus warned us not to allow the cares of life to choke out the Word. In light of the present-day economy, many are consumed with the cares of life. Concerning the cares of life that bog us down, Jesus stated, "*Now these are the ones sown among thorns; they are the ones who hear the word,; the cares of this world, the deceitfulness of riches, and the desires for other things entering in choke the word, and it becomes unfruitful*" (Mark 4:18, 19). But I have good news for you!

When we become intoxicated on the Helper, the Comforter, the Teacher, then the Holy Spirit will cause Christ's divine nature to be fully manifest in and through us as we yield ultimately to Him. We will be inebriated by God, and the cares of life will not touch us. Much persecution will come against those who fully embrace all the Holy Spirit provides us, but there will be great rewards! Creative miracles will explode, and if you thought you had seen all of God's signs and wonders, get ready for new ones!

Even as I am writing this, I am overcome by His thick, rich presence that I can scarcely write this due to the pleasure He is releasing in me right now. If you like, just reach out and take some for yourself right now.

A DIVIDING LINE

There will be a dividing line released in the earth, clearly separating those who want all God has to offer you from those who resist the Holy Spirit's supernatural life. If you are ready, God will usher in a glory and love movement that will cover the earth. Those who say yes to God and all He has to grant you will be given keys to see regional outpourings, and the winds of change will begin to blow and influence the surrounding culture.

Embrace all the Holy Spirit wants to bestow upon you and receive great grace right now for acceleration and deployment into the harvest fields through media, missions, and much more! Many are called, but few are chosen. Be part of the chosen few.

JUICY FRUIT

Many of you have struggled to produce the fruit of the Spirit, and even fruitful ministries have labored using their works and effort but let me show you a better way. Jesus said, *"I am the vine, you are the branches. He who remains in Me, and I in him, the same bears much fruit, for apart from Me you can do nothing* (John 15:5). You are a branch, and as you abide in Jesus and allow the thick sap that flows through His vine to your branch, then you will begin to produce the juiciest fruit you have ever imagined!

Let that sap flow straight from Jesus into your branch, producing a supernatural love in you, including supernatural joy, supernatural peace, and supernatural patience, kindness, goodness, faithfulness, and humility, and self-control.

Lose yourself in Him right now as you are reading this chapter. This will be so much fun, compared to the feeling of barrenness you may have carried in the past. God is going to stick to you like glue. Through intimacy, God will also impregnate you with new life, and your ministry will bear much fruit!

He wants to unlock and open a miracle ministry on the inside of you that you don't even know is there. You will be overtaken by supernatural boldness as you become a gateway for signs and wonders in the earth. You will be a living tabernacle of God and will use the keys of the Kingdom to implement His purpose, and plans on the earth, as it is in Heaven.

Remember, God is a lover, and He is looking for a burning, hot, fiery bride that He can fully possess and consume. He desires to give the keys to unlock the mysteries of His Kingdom and propel His body into the greatest awakening the earth has ever seen.

Let's pray:

Father, we pray You will wipe away shame from us and intoxicate us with Your divine love. Lord, let us shimmer with fresh light, love, confidence, and dignity as we daily live in Your presence. Establish grace in our hearts, not just knowing about Your grace but experiencing it in Your glory, and fully becoming new creations in Christ. We decree we are passionate people who do adventurous things, a fanatical people who step out of the known into the unknown, and a compassionate people who love with a fervor!

12

THE INFLUENCE OF DREAMS

THE AVERAGE HUMAN BEING SLEEPS ABOUT SEVEN HOURS A NIGHT which equates to one-third of a lifetime. With this much time invested, there will be times when your dreams have important messages and meaning.

Dreams are among the most vivid and unique conscious experiences one can have. The narrative power of a dream is well documented throughout history, from spiritually uplifting stories such as Jacob's dream to dream warnings like Joseph's dream of Herod's plans to kill the Christ child. Despite their cultural and personal importance, dreams remain as enigmatic as ever.

According to scientific studies, "Transcendent dreams were most likely to be followed by reports of spiritual release—i.e., the dreamer experienced "refreshing—even ecstatic—freedom from life's entanglements." After a significant loss, dreamers reported more nightmares at first, followed by existential dreams, and eventually transcendent dreams, as though the function of each dream type has a psychological priority corresponding to its chronological order. Thinking about dreams in this way could truly change how we understand how our mind works while we sleep."[1]

There are over 125 references to dreams and dreamers in the Bible, and God is still speaking to His creation through dreams. If dreams were not so important, God would not spend so much time in the Bible telling us who dreamed, why they had dreams, what He was saying to them in the dreams, and what He did as a result of those dreams. Every Christian can probably recall at least one time when they believed God spoke to them in a dream.

Two overlapping groups refer to dreams. "In one group are words that closely align with the English word "dream" and describe something that happens during sleep. This includes terms such as *ḥalôm* (Hebrew) and *onar* (Greek). A second group includes terms that generally mean "vision," as these words are related to verbs of sight."[2]

Dreams from God are usually very spiritual experiences that are not easily forgotten. They almost become a part of the heart and mind of the person receiving the dream.

The book of Job addresses his perspective about dreams in Job 33:14, 15: *"For God may speak in one way, or in another, yet man does not perceive it. In a dream, in a vision of the night, when deep sleep falls upon men, while slumbering on their beds..."*

Spiritual or biblical dreams do occur and happen for a reason; the only thing we need to figure out is for what purpose. There are times in my life when dreams encouraged me.

THE DREAM WARNING

One time, I was going through a period of great condemnation when Jesus appeared to me in a dream and showed me the twelve disciples while they were eating at the last supper. In the dream, he pointed to Peter and said, "I want you to learn from his life." If any man had felt more condemned, it was Peter who denied the Lord. God wanted me to know that there is no condemnation for those who are in Christ who walk according to the spirit and not according to the flesh (See Romans 8:1).

On another occasion, the Lord gave me an incredible dream. In the dream, Jesus appeared to me in front of an excessively big tree, and he was dressed as Robin Hood. He began to sing, very dramatically, the following words, "Many of you are going to deny me." Then a bunch of random Christians that were next to me quickly replied in unison, "No Lord, we will never deny you"

Interestingly enough, I had this dream during a time when great deception was released by the enemy, including specific camps in the body of Christ. One of the issues was doctrines that seemed to be borderline universalism, as exemplified by hyper-grace teaching that was causing many people to fall into a lifestyle of sin.

I could see that this was a warning from the Lord about people falling from grace. It amazes me how easily people are manipulated by teachers having itching ears. When you read the entire New Testament, you understand that the Lord requires us to live a lifestyle of holiness. I can guarantee you there's going to be many so-called Christians that will be in hell. These people assumed they had the liberty to keep living in sin when they did not have that freedom!

Once saved, always saved, is another deception from the enemy. There are situations when someone falls into sin, and trample on the Son of God's blood until they find themselves with no more chances for repentance and God gives them over to a reprobate mind.

Next in the dream, Jesus grabbed an arrow out of his quiver, and shot it northward into a large tree in front of us. He then asked if anyone could hit his arrow. I got so excited! Without hesitation, I reached in my quiver, pulled an arrow out, placed it correctly in the bow, pulled the arrow back, and shot the arrow. To my utter amazement, the arrow directly hit Jesus' arrow, and then both arrows intertwined each other and grew until it became a living branch.

I felt the Lord telling me not to miss the mark of abiding in Christ. He is the vine, and we are the branches, and apart from him we can do nothing (See John 15). Some will inevitably fail and fall if they do not abide in the vine of Christ. They will be led astray by every wind, and wave of doctrine because they did not nourish themselves on the sound doctrine of Jesus Christ (See 1 Timothy 4:6).

A CORDIAL MEETING AND IMPARTATION

Another time, I had an amazing dream encounter. I was surrounded by three young-looking persons, possibly in their mid-to-late thirties, and they were gathered together, looking at me, talking about me, as if they were there to meet me. I walked up to the three individuals, and they cordially introduced themselves. They did not tell me their names, but the man who seemed to be the leader of the three said to me in a very polite voice, "We know who you are Munday, and have been sent by the Lord to meet you."

My eyes opened with wonder. They went on to say, "We are from Heaven and in our lifetimes, we experienced, and were part of the Welsh Revival, and the Lord sent us to release the Welsh Revival anointing upon your life." I suddenly felt my heart gripped with love as I walked toward them to receive this honorable prayer and impartation.

As I got closer to them, I noticed that they were all shining with light. It reminds me of Jesus' words in Matthew 13:43, "*Then the righteous shall shine forth as the sun in the Kingdom of their Father. He that has ears, let him hear.*"

I stepped toward the man who prayed for me. He looked like he had been in Heaven's glory! His hair shined like gold, and his eyes were a deep crystal blue, deeper than I have ever seen, and was filled with an otherworldly peace, love, and joy. As he laid hands on me, he released the same anointing on me, including a mantle for revival, a revival that would cause entire nations to change. That anointing was the hallmark of the Welsh Revival.

As he was praying for me, I noticed that we were spinning around and around in the glory and I felt as if I was floating on air. This impartation is for now. He also began to pray this prayer for me, "Only the pure in heart can carry this anointing."

People who are yielded to Christ will walk in purity of heart and godly character. We desperately need today's leaders to have a spiritual quality of 'hearts with pure motives' who will be true fathers for this generation.

The Lord spoke to me as I received this impartation and took it into my very core: He is releasing this mantle upon whoever is hungry for it. I release it upon all the readers who want it right now in Jesus' precious name!

WELSH REVIVAL SPREADS TO THE NATIONS

The Welsh Revival lasted only one year, between 1904-1905. Although it only lasted a year, it was the most significant revival in Wales during the 20th century. This was a time of intense revival, influenced by the renown, Evan Roberts, a blacksmith who became a preacher.

Evan Roberts preached all over the land of Wales, and an estimated one hundred thousand souls were converted. The implications were monumental. It was one of the most dramatic revivals in terms of its effect on the population. It was a genuine awakening, a special visitation that reached far beyond the Welsh border, triggering a series of revivals in other countries.

"The impact of the Welsh Revival can be seen in that, according to one historian, as much as ten years after the revivals, 82.5 percent of those who attended them were yet members of churches, and for twenty years the churches of Wales were still filled, because of the Welsh revival."[3] It swept the rest of Britain, Scandinavia, parts of Europe, North America, the mission fields of India, the Orient, Africa, and Latin America.

It is what authentic revival produces – a contagious love that burns in the hearts of those affected by it, and that spreads like wildfire and changes other nations as a result. The Lord is saying that, "It is time for My people to arise and believe that My power in them can be used to disciple entire nations."

God gave me a series of dreams of me visiting nations. In

those dreams, he told me God will pour out His Spirit on those nations in a fresh way. The prophecy for Pakistan came from a dream I had and the other nations mentioned came from a prophecy originating from other dreams, "I am pouring out My Spirit mightily upon Pakistan, and Pakistan will burn brightly for many nations in the reaches of China and the Middle East! I will also visit Turkmenistan!"

"I am going to shake Thailand with My glory, and even royalty will heed the word of the Lord and be saved! I am going to shake Wales again, England and the entire UK, and France! I am going to shake Estonia! I am going to shake Iceland with revival fire! I am pouring out My Spirit in Jerusalem, and there will be a shift over the entire nation of Israel."

A FORGOTTEN REVIVALIST AND THE COMING REVIVAL

Though Evan Roberts was the most celebrated catalyst during the Welsh revival, unbeknownst to many, there was another prominent leader in the revival. His name was Joseph Jenkins.

"Several months before the revival began, Rev. Joseph Jenkins of New Quay was praying earnestly that a change might come over the churches of the area. One Sunday morning in February 1904, he held a prayer meeting for young people at his church and asked them to share how they viewed God. One boy said, "Jesus is the light of the world," to which Rev. Jenkins replied, "Yes, but what does He mean to you?" 20-year-old Florrie Evans rose to her feet and declared, "Rydw i'n caru Arglwydd Iesu Grist a'i holl galon" ("I love the Lord Jesus Christ with all of my heart"). Instantly, the Holy Spirit descended on the room, melting their hardened hearts. The young people started weeping and declaring their love for Jesus. Slowly but surely, this brokenness spread to the surrounding towns and villages to spread the flame of renewal and revival."[4]

People were changed in so many ways during this revival. The crime rate dropped, drunkards were reformed, and pubs reported losses in their businesses. Vulgar language disappeared and never returned to the lips of many. It was reported that the mining horses failed to understand the born-again miners who seemed to speak the new language of Zion without cursing and blasphemy.

Even football and rugby fans lost uninterest because of the light of new joy and the redirection of the newly converted lives. It triggered revival around the world, even the famous Azusa Street revival of 1906, which forever changed the landscape of 20th century Christianity. A deep hunger for the Word of God, and an unquenchable thirst for more of the Spirit of God began at an early age for Roberts. Evan was on fire for God and the fire spread throughout the land. Joy was another hallmark of this heavenly visitation, and it will be in our time, coupled with radical demonstrations of signs and wonders.

I believe that the entire family of God will arise at this hour with furious fire igniting a supernatural generation, not built on carnal, selfish empires, but established on the foundation of Christ, expanding the Kingdom of God, equipping people to reap the great harvest, similar to the outpouring during the Welsh revival.

"Oh, give thanks to the Lord, for He is good! For His mercy endures forever. Let the redeemed of the Lord say so, Whom He has redeemed from the hand of the enemy, and gathered out of the

lands, from the east and from the west, from the north and from the south. They wandered in the wilderness in a desolate way; they found no city to dwell in. Hungry and thirsty, their soul fainted in them. Then they cried out to the Lord in their trouble, and He delivered them out of their distresses. And He led them forth by the right way, that they might go to a city for a dwelling place" (Psalm 107:1-7).

I hear God saying, "At this hour I am releasing My Glory and entire cities will be dwelling places for My glory! I am releasing My glory on Great Britain and Europe! I am releasing My glory upon America! This is the time for the greatest move of God the world has ever seen!" God says, "Even as Psalm 107:5-6 is written, "Their soul fainted in them. Then they cried out to the Lord in their trouble, and He delivered them out of their distresses." God says, "Open your mouths, cry out just as Psalm 107 says. As oracles, begin to ask Me for this move of My Spirit for this generation in your nation!"

During the Welsh revival, some asked God to send more of His Spirit, and His Spirit, He sent! My good friend, James Goll, taught a class called, *"The Greatest Youth Awakening,"* In his book, *Prayer Storm,* Goll wrote these words. "At the age of 13, young Evan Roberts began to seek the Lord. At the age of 26, Revival came to his hometown. He taught the people to pray two simple prayers. 'Send the Spirit now for Jesus Christ's sake.' The second prayer was similar. 'Send the Spirit now more powerfully for Jesus Christ sake.'" Indeed, God's Spirit came down, and 100,000 souls were swept up into God's Kingdom.

Today, a cry is arising – "More Lord!" There must be a youth revolution as it was with Evan Roberts. Evan Roberts and many men and women of God lost their lives, only to find greatness in Heaven.

This last description of the revival perhaps sums it up best:

"It was plainly evident now to everybody that God had answered the agonizing prayers of His people and had sent a mighty spiritual upheaval. A sense of the Lord's presence was everywhere. His presence was felt in the homes, on the streets, in the mines, factories and schools and even in the drinking saloons. So great was His Presence felt that even the places of amusement and carousal became places of holy awe. Many were the instances of men entering taverns, ordering drinks and then turning on their heels and leaving them untouched. Wales up to this time was in the grip of football fever when tens of thousands of working-class men thought and talked only of one thing. They gambled also on the result of the games. Now the famous football players themselves got converted and joined the open-air street meetings to testify what glorious things the Lord had done for them. Many of the teams were disbanded as the players got converted and the stadiums were empty."

"On that Christmas Sunday in 1904, G. Campbell Morgan closed his sermon by saying this. Let no man hear of what happened in Wales and try to start it in his land. Why? Because no man started it in Wales! We cannot produce revival. We can only pray that God would be gracious to us and send it in abundance!"[5]

Let's pray and believe it for our time, in Jesus' holy name!

Oh, that men would give thanks to the Lord for His goodness and His wonderful works to the children of men! For He satisfies the longing soul and fills the hungry soul with goodness (Psalm 107:8-9).

13

SOUL WINNER

The fruit of the righteous is a tree of life, and he that wins souls is wise (Proverbs 11:30).

Those who are wise shall shine like the brightness of the firmament, and those who turn many to righteousness like the stars forever and ever (Daniel 12:3).

IN 1903 THE CELEBRATED, CHARLES HADDON SPURGEON'S publisher, Passmore & Alabaster, published *The Soul Winner.* The book is a series of edited lectures to students and pastors about a passion that was central to Spurgeon's view of the Christian life and to the secret of his success: communicating Christ to others.[1]

The work is full of insights into Spurgeon's personal priorities in life and ministry. It is an obvious clue as to why he was able to build the world's largest evangelical church of the 19th century. "If John Calvin was the greatest theologian of the church, Jonathan Edwards the greatest philosopher, and George Whitefield the greatest evangelist, Spurgeon surely ranks as its greatest preacher."[2]

One man never stood in a pulpit, week after week, year after year, for almost four decades, and preached the gospel with greater worldwide success and lasting impact than Spurgeon. To this day, he remains "the Prince of Preachers."

"Though he deeply loved theology, Spurgeon stated, "I would sooner bring one sinner to Jesus Christ than unpack all the mysteries of the divine Word." He reveled in seeking the salvation of the lost. Here is how Spurgeon described the central importance of evangelism in his ministry: *I would rather be the means of saving a soul from death than be the greatest orator on earth. I would rather bring the poorest woman in the world to the feet of Jesus than I would be made Archbishop of Canterbury. I would sooner pluck one single brand from the burning than explain all mysteries."* [3]

"Spurgeon opens his message with these words. "Soulwinning is the chief business of the Christian minister; indeed, it should be the main pursuit of every true believer. We should each say with Simon Peter, "I go a fishing," and with Paul our aim should be, "That I might by all means save some."[4]

"You preach, brethren, with this object, that men may quit their sins, and fly to Christ for pardon, that by His blessed Spirit they may be renovated, and become as much in love with everything that is holy as they are now in love with everything that is sinful. You aim at a radical cure; the axe is laid at the root of the trees; the amendment of the old nature would not content you, but you seek for the imparting, by a divine power, of a new nature, that those who gather round you in the streets may live unto God."[5]

"The salvation of one soul is worth more than the framing of a Magna Charta of a thousand worlds."[6]

THE INFLUENCE OF SPIRITUAL FATHERS

It seems like the drunker I am in the Holy Spirit, the more he releases fresh revelation in my life, including dreams and visions. I remember the dream I received by the Holy Spirit right before I was privileged to meet prophet Bob Jones, which was a few years before he passed away.

My good friend, Jeff Jansen, took me to the green room during a conference he was hosting at his church. He wanted to introduce me to Bob Jones. This was the season of my life when I was in the Holy Spirit for weeks. The Spirit was anointing my wife and I, during a season when God started promoting our ministry. Our platform launched to another level as we were fathering this generation.

When I walked into the green room, Jeff introduced me to Bob saying, "Hey Bob, this is..." Before he could say my name, Bob interrupted Jeff and exclaimed, "You're a soul winner, you're a soul winner, and your job is to be on the streets winning souls to Jesus!" I agreed with him and received the prophet's blessing. I rejoice that I am now living that prophecy every single day of my life as we continue to take Jesus to the streets. While spending time with him that weekend, I was so enriched by the glory of God on this man of God that I dearly held in high esteem.

Truthfully, I do not consider myself one of Bob Jones' spiritual sons because I did not walk with him like others. However, I do consider Jeff Jansen and James Goll as my spiritual fathers, who Bob Jones mentored. I received that mantle of impartation from them, making me sort of a grandson. It is an honor having these men of God in my life, as they cheer me on for the kingdom!

HOLY SPIRIT DOVES

That same weekend I shared with Bob Jones a dream I had. In the dream, I found myself in what looked like an older church made of wood with rafters above me. I kneeled at the altar and entered into prayer, when I noticed doves sitting on the church rafters.

The doves were there to make sure I did not sit still. When I would sit still, they would swoop down and fly all around me, pecking every part of my body. It was not painful but irritating enough to make me know I should get up and move! They would gracefully fly up to the rafters and then repeat the process all over again, until I got up and moved! When I shared the dreams with Bob Jones, he told me that those are the Holy Spirit doves, assigned over my life to make sure I did not sit still, and got up and moved into my calling for evangelism.

Sadly, many people hear of other people's dreams, like this one, and think that they should wait on a dream from God, telling them they must go to the streets. It is a regular mistake people make inside the prophetic movement. They wait for a word from God but never pick up the word of God. If you read the word of God, the message is clear that you should go into all the world, and make disciples, baptizing them in the name of the Father, the Son and the Holy Spirit (See Matthew 28:19, 20). You do not need a word from God to do what the word of God instructs you to do.

The Holy Spirit doves are coming to peck you and tell you it is time to get moving. If we move, the angels will move! If we get up and go preach, all of heaven will come and move with us.

BURNING HEARTS

I loved the story of the road to Emmaus when the disciples encountered a stranger who enthralled them. The two disciples of Jesus were walking along the narrow country road leading to Emmaus, located just a short distance west from Jerusalem. The road stretches along the Judean Mountains' scenic rolling hills amidst the deep green of local pines, oaks, and other native brush.

As they traveled, a stranger joined them and asked them what they were talking about. While walking and talking, they proceeded to tell the stranger about the recent events in Jerusalem, highlighting the story of Jesus' crucifixion and resurrection. Jesus entered the conversation sharing with them, from the scriptures, things concerning himself, starting with Moses and then all the prophets. Throughout the conversation, they had no clue that the stranger was Jesus. Once they entered Emmaus, they encouraged Jesus to have a meal with them. After he broke the bread and gave it to the disciples, their eyes were opened, and they recognized the stranger was Jesus. When he disappeared, they excitedly responded, *"They said to each other, "Did not our hearts burn within us while he talked to us on the road, while he opened to us the Scriptures?"* (Luke 24:32).

The amazing thing is that the words of the disciples, "Did not our hearts burn within us?" became a theme of our ministry. When you dig deeper into a personal relationship with Jesus, you radically put his teachings into practice, and your heart begins to burn for him! Every wonderful thing this world totes as the next greatest thing pales in comparison to spending time in the presence of Jesus and taking his gospel to the streets.

During the COVID-19 crisis, I still went out every day and was shocked at how many believers lived in fear. It felt like we were the only ones preaching the gospel on the streets. When our hearts burn within us, no plague in the earth can stop us from propagating to other this incredible and life-changing message of the good news!

Ask yourself right now what it will take to realize that this life is just a vapor and, therefore how important it is to give Jesus Christ everything you have. God is about to send his Holy Spirit doves to the body of Christ, and they will lovingly pick on his children and say, "Hey you! That's right, I said you! I need you to get to work!" When you get to work, the angels will get to work because they're waiting for you to do something!

LOSE YOUR LIFE, FIND YOUR LIFE

I often wonder if God connected me with such amazing people like James Goll, Jeff Jansen, and Patricia King because of the times I've burned in my heart for Jesus. I remember those times when I fasted every other day of my life, seeking heaven with all my heart! I remember the times I laid down my life, and I served spiritual leaders, while not asking for a salary, simply trusting God to bring us Partners for our mission trips.

If you lose your life as you know it, you will find it. I lost my life serving others, and I found a ministry that God fit me into, like a shoe walking with the prophets, because he saw a burning heart that wanted to waste it on Jesus.

I went to church for years, cleaning toilets, mowing lawns, while praying for doors to open up to the nations! God is a rewarder of those who diligently seek him, and I can tell you it is true if you want to become great, you need to become the least of all. During vacation bible school, I got up early in the morning working tirelessly and setting up rooms for little kids to come and receive the Holy Spirit. For years, my wife and I worked around the clock as interns and serving as mission directors of our local church, while also leading the worship team. The kingdom of God is compiled of the least, the last, and the lost. That's who I am, and that's my market.

All that time, I dreamed of the day when God would see me serving and then reward me with the full-time ministry because my heart was broken for souls. We need to learn these things first before we go to heaven.

In heaven we will still be serving each other, and we will all be equal. We must learn to treat each member of the body of Christ-like precious pearls of great price. Treat others like they are, the treasure in a field, and as Jesus said, "Sell everything to buy the field with your treasure" (Mathew 13:44). Ask God to give you a greater determination to waste your life on Jesus so you can find life more abundant than what it was before.

The great divide is coming. Some fully yield to the Holy Spirit, and others will quench him. While writing this book, we are nearing Pentecost, and I hear the Lord's yes, and amen. The eyes of the Lord go to and fro throughout all the earth, and He is seeking those who belong entirely to Him and looking for those who will not compromise and refuse to quench His companionship.

As I wrote in the introduction, this book can inspire and make your wildest dreams come true. For some of you, this is new, and maybe for many, you already heard this, but the fire has gone out, and you know it deep inside. Perhaps you let the fire flicker and fade when you slowly began to accept the things of the world. Back in the recesses of your mind and heart, you saw it as normal everyday life. I remind you that the spirit of this world is strong and dangerous if you give it any room. However, on a higher note, there are no limits to your experiences in the realms of the Holy Spirit when you fall on your face before him and say, "Lord, your will be done."

SERVING AND HONORING ONE ANOTHER

"Instead, whoever wants to be great among you must be your servant, and whoever wants to be first must be your slave" (Matthew 20:26-27). In this hour, the Lord emphasized this Scripture for me and I believe it will be a refreshing word for you causing hope to spring forth in your personal lives.

The tape measure that this world utilizes to define greatness means little in the eyes of God. Paul noted this in 1 Corinthians 1:26, *"For ye see your calling, brethren, how that not many wise men after the flesh, not many mighty, not many noble, are called."*

When the heavenly standards of greatness, as established by Christ, is juxtaposed with the world's standards, we are faced with a defined disparity. The secular culture defines greatness with words like accomplishments and accolades, wealth and status, brands and platforms, and power and beauty. The culture of the kingdom defines greatness with these contrasting words like humility and servanthood, selflessness and faithfulness, repentant and loyal, and the love of others.

Who is the greatest of all? Two verses answer the question.

Whoever therefore shall humble himself as this little child, the same is greatest in the kingdom of heaven (Mathew 18:4). The one who is the remotest from pride and ambition and does not make superiority their priority are the greatest in God's kingdom.

For whether is greater, he that sits at meat, or he that serves? is not he that sits at meat? but I am among you as he that serves (Luke 22;27). He, the admittedly greater, had assumed the position of the less by becoming a servant. In His kingdom, power is to be used to help others, not to glorify oneself. The way to greatness is to become small, and to serve, becoming a servant of servants. The Jews expected a conquering king, but King Jesus came with a towel.

Real greatness places value on things overlooked and overseen. It is birthed in a childlike desire to share, dream, and help build a scaffolding for others' dreams to come true. Greatness in the kingdom is identified with those who ease the burdens of another without recognition or recompense. Parabolically speaking, greatness in heaven, forged in unprecedented wisdom, inspires us to take on the lowly cloak of humility – knowing that something greater and weightier of substance is in our future.

"Who, although He existed in the form of God, did not regard equality with God a thing to be grasped, but emptied Himself, taking the form of a bond-servant, and being made in the likeness of men" (Philippians 2:6, 7, NASV). Not clutching his equality with God, Jesus stripped himself in the incarnation and became a

servant. In humility, he took on human flesh and did not come to be served, but to serve, in dissimilarity to the ways of this world.

Through the matrix of servanthood, God initiates a shift in the church culture activated by the servanthood of the saints, causing a beautiful reformation in this church age. The highest level of glory will be revealed through a people of unity while serving and honoring one another. Too much of today's church culture does the opposite. Behind the titles of apostles or other five-fold titles, there is a power lust that manifests itself in ambitious self-promotion, leading to worshiping them rather than Jesus. This must end! When we reach heaven, Jesus will call us by our name, not our title, and he will ask us how much we loved and served others.

Many have been tested in their relationships but overcame discord by forgiveness and casting the root of bitterness through a servant's heart. Some have failed but remember how Jesus taught His disciples to learn through their failures. Now is not the time to throw in the towel and quit like Peter when he denied his Lord. It is time to stand up and remember what the Lord has spoken over you in the past, and as you embrace that word, take your place in history.

A famous pastor once enlightened me to see an army from around the world and they were going through the hardest trials of their lives. I hear them blaming the enemy; however, I see it is not always the enemy. The Lord has many faithful servants in spiritual boot camp, and God is raising an army of resistance for the coming days. This company of servants cannot be bought, cannot be shaken, and will not bow down to the spirit of this world. These are the sons of light God is bringing to the forefront of the world stage, and on that stage, they will shine brightly during the darkest hours.

A BEACON OF LIGHT

I hear the Lord saying, "I am raising a servant army! During this season, many of you had to lay down or, at least, downsize your work, or possibly your ministry, while putting your dreams on hold, so that you could fight for others. They may be people in your own family or friends of yours. There is a grace in provision as I am putting personal houses in order. Those entire families will be a beacon of hope and light for the church and the world. I am placing greater emphasis on family right now, healing families to bring light to the world. My church is not a building, a program, or an institution, but a powerful living family that serves each other and the living Christ. This is why our ministry is now focusing more on raising up discipleship making groups with discovery Bible studies that can reach neighborhoods."

Many of you were forced to find gold and other things of spiritual value that were overlooked, like in the everyday things, including the seemingly trivial labor you have faithfully done. Some feel like you were pushed to the sidelines, doing what appears to be currently irrelevant in the eyes of others. Many of you have giftings inside you that you feel has been neglected by others while faithfully serving people with smiles on your face but shedding unrelenting tears in the secret place.

Through all this heartache, the Lord will open many eyes to see the beauty of a humble 'manger style ministry' by what He is producing upon you. It has and will have more power and affluence than a mighty empire and proves that their labor will bear the greatest fruit. Be encouraged, you are building something eternal that cannot be measured, it cannot be weighed, and it cannot be broken.

God reminded me of a Scripture that is key to revealing His beautiful future for you, generous, noble, and kingly! *"For nothing is concealed that won't be revealed, and nothing hidden that won't be made known and come to light"* (Luke 8:17). Get ready, honor is coming for you! If no one notices or sees it, be assured that heaven sees your labor of love. Remember, your patience will be rewarded. There is a palace God has in mind for us, even when we feel we have been thrown into a pit. In Father's house, there are many mansions (John 14:2).

David's testimony can become your story. *"I had fainted, unless I had believed to see the goodness of the LORD in the land of the living. Wait on the LORD: be of good courage, and He shall strengthen your heart: wait, I say, on the LORD"* (Psalms 27:13, 14).

In Romans 5:3-5, the apostle Paul gives directions for those in times of trouble, *"Not only so, but we also glory in our sufferings, because we know that suffering produces perseverance; perseverance, character; and character, hope. And hope does not put us to shame, because God's love has been poured out into our hearts through the Holy Spirit, who has been given to us."*

May God richly bless you. A servant army is rising, and you are called to be a part of it, and God the Father is so proud of you! Keep going and never give up in Jesus' precious name. Let's lose our lives in Jesus and find them in His precious name!

Finally, if you feel you have hidden intentional sin in your life after reading this book, let me biblically say that you are gambling with your eternal destiny. If you want to experience eternal life, repent from your sins and put your trust in Jesus

Christ right now! Don't wait another day. The cross of Jesus, His blood, and His body will be enough if you follow and obey Him. Once doing so, radically obey his teachings and make disciples. Develop a love for the lost Jewish people and also for the Gentiles. I encourage you to subscribe to Mission Frontiers magazine to learn how to make disciples and become a part of the discipleship making movement. Feel free to email our ministry for some personal advice on starting discipleship making home meetings in your community. Do these things and you can experience Ecstatic Christianity today!

MEET THE AUTHOR

Munday and Jennifer Martin are the founders of Contagious Love International. They are prophetic healing evangelists based in the Nashville, TN area. Munday was radically saved in 1999 shortly after he encountered a dream from the Lord where he saw a glimpse of both Heaven and Hell in the middle of the night while lost in college. After this incredible encounter, Munday gave his life to Jesus and was called into a global impacting ministry to the nations with a ravished love for His Savior.

They are committed to preaching the gospel of Jesus Christ to America and the nations, equipping a supernatural Jesus generation who will manifest miraculous lives to impact communities and culture. Munday and Jennifer both minister and preach in the Glory, blazing a trail of reformation, miracles, healings, signs and wonders, and intense outbreaks of the glory of God in churches, conferences, crusades, and the streets in the US and the nations, leading many into the fullness of God.

Munday Martin was ordained in 2008 as a "new breed" Apostolic and Prophetic Revivalist for this generation by Dr. and Prophet James Goll of Encounters Network, author of "The Seer." Munday and Jennifer were both ordained in 2009 by Jeff Jansen of Global Fire Ministries, author of "Glory Rising."

Munday and Jennifer also are now active members of Jeff Jansen's Global Connect under the leadership of Jeff Jansen and Munday and Jennifer are also members of Che Ahn's apostolic network called H.I.M., a coalition of church leaders and ministries around the world.

Contagious Love International's Board of Apostolic Advisors

- James Goll of *Encounters Network*
- Mickey Robinson of *Prophetic Destiny International*
- Pastor Jerry Bryant Nashville Tennessee

For more information visit:
www.contagiousloveintl.com

ACKNOWLEDGMENTS

Thanks to David Joseph for the beautifully designed cover.

Appreciation to Don Milam, the fanciful ghostwriter and editor of my book.

ENDNOTES

INTRODUCTION

1. David Orr, *You're Probably Misreading Robert Frost's Most Famous Poem,* https://lithub.com/youre-probably-misreading-robert-frosts-most-famous-poem/ Accessed June 5, 2020
2. David Orr, *You're Probably Misreading Robert Frost's Most Famous Poem, Ibid,* Accessed June 5, 2020
3. Ellicott"s Commentary for English Readers, https://biblehub.com/commentaries/jeremiah/6-16.htm, Accessed June 5, 2020

1. THE ART OF GETTING LOST

1. https://www.goalcast.com/2019/06/19/brene-brown-quotes/, Accessed June 6, 2020
2. https://parade.com/1018534/lindsaylowe/brene-brown-quotes/, Accessed June 6, 2020
3. Gill's Exposition of the Entire Bible, https://biblehub.com/commentaries/acts/1-8.htm, Accessed June 7, 2020

2. FIRST ADAM, LAST ADAM

1. S.D. Gordon, *Quiet Talks on Jesus* (Destiny Image, Shippensburg, Pa, 2005) 60
2. Jacob Boehme, http://www.passtheword.org/Jacob-Boehme/jbimage2.htm, Accessed June 8, 2020
3. *The Rock,* T.S. Eliot, http://www.roy-hart.com/rock.htm, Accessed June 8, 2020
4. https://www.pinterest.com/CandidChristian/watchman-nee-quotes/, Accessed June 10, 2020
5. John R.W. Stott, *In Christ: The Meaning and Implications of the Gospel of Jesus Christ,* https://www.cslewisinstitute.org/In_Christ_page1, Accessed June 10, 2020
6. https://www.ligonier.org/blog/what-church/, Accessed June 10, 2020

7. Barnes Notes of the Bible, Alfred Barnes, https://biblehub.com/commentaries/matthew/13-44.htm, June 12, 2020

3. LOSE MY UNBELIEF, FIND GREATER FAITH

1. Bill Johnson, *When Heaven Invades Earth,* https://www.goodreads.com/work/quotes/73860-when-heaven-invades-earth, Accessed June 20, 2020
2. John Wesley, https://www.seedbed.com/on-john-wesley-quotes/, Accessed June 20, 2020

5. AS YOU GO, PREACH

1. Sesame Street, *People in Your Neighborhood,* https://www.metrolyrics.com/people-in-your-neighborhood-lyrics-sesame-street.html, Accessed June 27, 2020
2. https://biblehub.com/commentaries/luke/16-9.htm, Accessed June 27, 2020
3. Sam Storms, *The Christian and Repentance,* https://www.thegospelcoalition.org/essay/the-christian-and-repentance/, Accessed June 28, 2020

6. THE ECSTASY OF LOVING YOUR HATERS

1. William Nessel, *The Transforming Power of Love,* https://www.hprweb.com/2015/12/the-transforming-power-of-love/, Accessed July 3, 2020
2. https://biblehub.com/commentaries/romans/12-20.htm, Accessed July 3, 2020

7. LOSING YOURSELF IN JESUS

1. Mel Tari, Heart of God Ministries, http://heartaftergodministries.net/mel-tari/, Accessed July 6, 2020
2. https://caldronpool.com/desire-nothing-world-can-satisfy/, accessed July 7, 2020
3. Expositor's Greek New Testament, https://biblehub.com/commentaries/matthew/13-33.htm, Accessed July 7, 2020

8. THE DELICIOUS FRUIT OF THE SPIRIT

1. Parker J. Palmer, *Let Your Life Speak,* https://www.themuse.com/advice/how-to-find-the-answer-to-what-do-i-want-to-do-with-my-life, Accessed July 14, 2020
2. Process Spirituality, Doing versus Being, https://bible.org/seriespage/2-process-spirituality-being-versus-doing, Accessed July 14, 2020
3. Viktor Frankl, *Yes to Life,* (Beacon Press, Boston, 2019) 22, 50
4. http://eerdword.com/2016/09/19/what-do-you-seek-the-questions-of-jesus-as-challenge-and-promise/, Accessed July 14, 2020
5. Youth for Christ, *The Struggle is Over,* http://www.songlyrics.com/youth-for-christ/the-struggle-is-over-lyrics/, Accessed July 16, 2020

9. EXCHANGING LIFELESS CHRISTIANITY FOR POWER

1. https://documentedhealings.com/14-quotes-smith-wigglesworth-healing/, Accessed July 25, 2020
2. https://www.lyrics.com/artist/atom, Accessed July 24, 2020
3. C.S. Lewis Institute, John R.W. Stott, "In Christ" *The Meaning and Implications of the Gospel of Jesus Christ,* https://www.cslewisinstitute.org/In_Christ_page1, Accessed July 24, 2020
4. J. M. Whiton, Ph. D., The Bible Illustrator, https://biblehub.com/sermons/auth/whiton/in_god.htm, Accessed July 24, 2020

10. A NEW ERA IN THE BODY OF CHRIST

1. Brian Houston, https://brianchouston.com/2016/06/22/behold-i-do-a-new-thing/, Accessed July 28, 2020
2. https://biblehub.com/commentaries/ephesians/4-13.htm, Accessed July 30, 2020

11. JUICY FRUIT

1. https://biblehub.com/commentaries/galatians/5-22.htm, Accessed July 31, 2020

12. THE INFLUENCE OF DREAMS

I. Julia Barsik, *The Influence of Dreams,* https://greatergood.berkeley.edu/article/item/the_influence_of_dreams/, Accessed August 14, 2020

2. https://blog.logos.com/2020/07/what-do-dreams-in-the-bible-mean-these-9-words-reveal-hints/, Accessed August 14, 2020

3. https://www.5minutesinchurchhistory.com/the-welsh-revivals/, Accessed August 14, 2020

4. http://www.pisgahchapel.com/wp-content/uploads/2016/05/Flier-The1904WelshRevivalv4.pdf, Accessed August 14, 2020

5. Sam Storms, 10 Things You Should Know About the Welsh Revival of 1904-06, https://www.samstorms.org/enjoying-god-blog/post/10-things-you-should-know-about-the-welsh-revival-of-1904-06, Accessed August 14, 2020

13. SOUL WINNER

I. Steven Lawson, *Charles Spurgeon: The Heart of a Soul-Winner,* https://www.ligonier.org/blog/charles-spurgeon-heart-soul-winner/ Accessed August 17, 2020

2. Lex Loizides, https://lexloiz.wordpress.com/book-reviews/ch-spurgeon-the-soul-winner/,Accessed August 17, 2020

3. Steven Lawson, *Charles Spurgeon: The Heart of a Soul-Winner,* https://www.ligonier.org/blog/charles-spurgeon-heart-soul-winner/ Accessed August 17, 2020

4. Charles Haddon Spurgeon, *The Soul Winner,* page 3, eBook edition, http://thesoulwinner.org/ebooks/The%20Soul%20Winner%20-%20Spurgeon.pdf, Accessed August 17, 2020

5. Charles Haddon Spurgeon, *The Soul Winner,* page 86, ebook edition, http://thesoulwinner.org/ebooks/The%20Soul%20Winner%20-%20Spurgeon.pdf, Accessed August 17, 2020

6. Keble (name unknown), https://archive.spurgeon.org/misc/soulwinr.php, August 17, 2020

Made in the USA
Middletown, DE
16 November 2020